Ten Parables of Jesus
WORKBOOK

Ten Parables of Jesus
WORKBOOK

by Jamie Buckingham

Studies in the Gospels of Ten Parables of Jesus Christ

To be used with "Ten Parables of Jesus"
Video Tape Series

CONTENTS

Ten Parables of Jesus

1. Truth is always simple.
2. The Bible is God's Word to us today.
3. Accepting the teachings of Jesus will change your life.
4. Parables teach us about God—and about ourselves.
5. God is much bigger than we think He is.

Ten Parables of Jesus

INTRODUCTION

Read This First

God has many ways of teaching us. Jesus taught by example. Men looked at how He lived, and decided to walk that way also.

He also taught by precept. By that I mean He often spoke directly to people. We might even call it preaching.

But His favorite way of teaching was through the use of the parable. He loved to tell stories—stories with spiritual meanings.

In the fall of 1987, I visited Israel with a video camera crew. I wanted to go to ten of the sites where Jesus told his best-known parables. I had long suspected that Jesus used visual things when telling these stories. When He told the story of the good shepherd, He pointed to a shepherd with his flock of sheep in a nearby pasture. When He told the parable of the sower and the seed, he was probably sitting on a rock beside a field where a farmer was sowing his spring seed. Jesus was a man of the earth, and He used earthy things to convey spiritual truth.

Standing on the sites where I felt Jesus taught, I video-taped the brief messages which accompany these lessons.

This workbook has been designed to be used with those taped video messages. The workbook will be best used in a small group of people who have a leader (teacher or instructor). Ideal usage calls for the same group to meet once a week for ten weeks. You'll need your Bible, because the questions in the workbook are all taken from the various scriptural accounts of Jesus' parables—plus a number of related passages. Each session should last about an hour and should begin as the group views the section of the video tape pertaining to the chapter to be studied. Each video segment runs about 12 minutes. Then the teacher will take over, using this workbook as a guide, and lead the class in a study of the material at hand.

When this material was first produced some people complained that the video teaching segments were not long enough. However, I believe that while video is an important teaching tool (you could never see what I saw without it), it is not a substitute for the personalization brought by a teacher, a workbook, and a Bible.

What I have given you is the best of both methods.

Several years ago I produced a similar set of video tapes and a workbook called "The Journey to Spiritual Maturity." In it I traced the footsteps of Moses through the Sinai, pausing to teach along the way. Shortly after that material was distributed I began getting letters from prison and jail chaplains—as well as Bible study leaders who were working with men and women behind bars. They were saying the material was ideal for prison Bible studies since it combined the visual (video) with the written (workbook) with an instructor. Video alone is not sufficient to convey truth. It must be combined with the personal touch of a teacher to answer—and ask—questions, and a workbook to stimulate actual Bible reading and study.

Encouraged that prisoners were using the material, I prepared three more series using the same technique. One series covered "Ten Miracles of Jesus." Another was called "Ten Bible People Like Me," and was a study of ten Bible heroes. This one looks at "Ten Parables of Jesus." All were designed—my teaching on location in Israel as well as the workbooks—to be used in prisons and jails where hundreds of thousands of men and women are eagerly learning more about God.

However, it soon became evident that what is good for prisoners is good for all. Thus the material was slightly modified so it can be used just as easily by a Sunday school class or a home group as by a prison Bible study group.

As you study these parables of Jesus, the same Holy Spirit Who inspired Jesus in the telling will go to work in your own life to give you spiritual understanding. The purpose of this workbook is to stimulate you, excite you, change you by bringing you to the place where you will see the parables of Jesus were not just for yesterday—they are for today. They were not just for those people who heard Jesus in person, they are for you.

A parable is nothing more than a story—a story with a hidden, or not so hidden, meaning.

Jesus was a storyteller. He was a Master storyteller. Unlike most storytellers, however, He did not tell his stories to entertain. He told stories to teach. He wanted His listeners to learn about God, about God's Kingdom, about God's Son, and about themselves. The stories He told were filled with humor, common sense, biting satire, and deep spiritual truth. They prodded. They stimulated. They answered questions. They raised questions. But always, they pointed men toward God's highest way for the lives of the listeners.

In this study of these ten parables of Jesus you'll visit the sites where Jesus was when He told these marvelous stories. On the video tape you'll stand with me high above the ruins of an ancient inn along the notorious road from Jerusalem to Jericho where a despised Samaritan stopped to render aid—after the religious people had passed by.

You'll go with me into one of those ancient stone towers in the middle of an olive grove. There the father, in Jesus' story of the prodigal son, stood and waited for his rebellious son to come walking down the long road home.

You'll come with me down into the bottom of a deep wadi—or canyon—where Jesus might have stood as He told the story of the two houses—one built on rock and the other on the sand of the canyon bottom.

You'll also travel with me to the famous Western Wall, also called the Wailing Wall. This is the last remaining portion of the old Temple in Jerusalem. It was here Jesus stood when He told his touching, but troublesome, story of the two men who went up to the temple to pray: one a Pharisee, another a publican. It was a pointed story, poking holes in the religious balloons of the Pharisees.

But once the video is off, the real fun begins. It is then you will open your Bible and begin to study these parables for yourself. Not just to learn what Jesus said—but to discover what He is still saying. And most important, what He is saying to you.

Are you a rebellious prodigal, determined to do things your own way? Are you an arrogant, self-righteous elder brother who is angry because of what seems to be injustice? Or do you reflect the wisdom, patience, and mercy of a loving Father?

Like I said, you'll meet yourself in every one of these parables. And hopefully, the person you see will then call out to God for change and growth.

Therefore, if you don't need to change, if you are totally satisfied with yourself, if you don't need to grow, if you have all the answers (or even most of them) when it comes to life—then beware. These parables will grab you and turn you every which way but loose.

But if you are one of those folks who are hungry and thirsty for righteousness— these parables will fill you, change you. At least they'll introduce you to the One who does change you. And He will be so attractive you'll rush to invite Him into your life in a new way.

Welcome to the wonderful world of the story. Welcome into the wonderful heart of the Storyteller.

Jamie Buckingham
Melbourne, Florida

GETTING THE MOST FROM THIS STUDY

Using the accompanying video tapes this workbook is designed to lead you, step by step, into an understanding of the meaning and the nature of the parables of Jesus. In particular you will be studying ten of His best known parables. The video segments of these lessons were taped on the locations in Israel where He actually taught—using as object lessons the things around Him: sheep, farmers, and houses. You will see the Sea of Galilee, the courtyard of a Jewish house, the Wailing Wall of the Temple where the Orthodox Jews pray in public, the Good Samaritan Inn, and a deep, mysterious, wadi (canyon) in the Judean wilderness where Jesus warned against building your house in the wrong place. You will be as much a part of the audience as the group of people who accompanied the camera crew when the tapes were made.

Those parables of Jesus—as simple yet profound as they were—are still speaking to the hearts of all those who have "ears to hear," as Jesus was fond of saying. It is my prayer that, as you study these marvelous teachings in your Bible and answer the questions in this workbook, you too, will allow God's Spirit to speak directly to your heart, changing your understanding of God and improving the quality of your life and ministry on earth.

The material on the video tape and in this workbook can be used in a number of different ways. It can be the basis of an individual study. It can be used in a small group, such as a Bible study group, a Sunday school class, or a house group. Experience has shown the greatest benefit will come when a group of people study the material together under a leader who is well-prepared on the subject.

Helps for the Leader

If you are a leader preparing to take a group of people into a study on the parables of Jesus, you should consider the following:

1. Necessary Materials

* A good color television set with a screen large enough to be seen by all present.

* A reliable video player.

* A power source within reach of the plugs for the TV and VCR.

* Comfortable seating so each person may see the TV screen and the teacher.

* A Bible for each student. The workbook uses Scripture quotes from the New International Version (NIV), but any Bible will do.

* A workbook for each student.

* Pen or pencil for each student.

Although parallel reading is not mandatory, it is helpful. I have written a book titled *Ten Parables of Jesus—Poking Holes in Religious Balloons*—which is designed to be used with this course. Published by Paraclete Press, Orleans, Massassachusets, it is a basic Bible commentary on the same parables covered in this study, illustrated with modern day applications similar to the ones used by Jesus. The book covers, in much greater detail, all the material presented in this course, as well as a wealth of other background information.

2. Preparation

Before teaching others you should not only view the entire video series—all 10 segments—but you should work your way through this workbook. You will find a number of Scripture references. Study them in depth before attempting to lead the class in discussion. You are not expected to have all the answers. Your job will be to help the students ask the right questions and stimulate them to explore the Bible for themselves.

3. Be Aware

As you lead the class be aware that each person present is going through some kind of crisis in his or her life to which these parables will speak directly. This could be a financial crisis, a grief experience, a problem with personal identification, a battle with demons or temptation, a crisis in the home, spiritual confusion, or a number of different mountains which seem too high to climb and too thick to tunnel through. Your awareness of their special needs will help when it comes to answering questions and leading in discussion. Do not be afraid to pause, at any place in the discussion, and minister to that person or persons—asking the class to join in as the Holy Spirit applies the truth of God to the lives of those who have "ears to hear."

4. Stick to the Subject

Your job, as teacher, is to hold the discussion to the subject of the parable being taught. There will always be those in the class who will want to lead you on some rabbit chase down a side path, will want to monopolize the discussion, or try to entice you into an argument over some minor point. It is important that you stick, as nearly as possible, to the outline of the subject at hand. The material has been carefully designed to build principle on principle with the eventual aim of the student becoming "thoroughly equipped for every good work" (II Timothy 3:17). Do not preach. Do not monopolize the conversation yourself. Do not allow the class to drift from the subject matter.

5. Stimulate Discussion

Remember, your job as teacher is not to give answers—even if you know them—but to skillfully stimulate discussion and encourage each student to find God's Word for his own life. The Holy Spirit will help you, for He not only wants each student to understand these parables of Jesus, He wants each one to let the life-changing truth of each story bring him to a place of resolution. Do not limit yourself to the material covered in this workbook. It is merely a guide, a primer for discussion. Allow the Holy Spirit to direct your class sessions.

6. Be Sensitive to Time

If your class has more than an hour for each study, arrange for a break of a few minutes for refreshment or a stretch. If the group discussion is dynamic, or if someone in the class indicates a need for personal ministry, you may want to keep the session going. Or, if the particular subject is stimulating extra discussion, you may want to put off the next segment in order to continue this one for an additional week. For instance, the parable of the talents can hardly be contained in one session. If that is the case, I recommend the class review the same video segment at the opening of the second week of study to stimulate continuing discussion.

Remember, just because the class has ended does not mean the Holy Spirit will not continue to work. In fact, in all probability the greatest work of the Spirit in the lives of the students will take place after the class is over. That means you may want to open the next class with a brief report on the Spirit's activity since the class last met.

Helps for Students

Before you start this course ask yourself these questions:

* Am I really committed to finding God's will for my life?

* Am I willing to commit myself to attend all the sessions of this course unless unavoidably detained?

* Am I willing to open my mind to new truth beyond what I now believe?

* Am I willing to prepare ahead of time through prayer and by reading my Bible and doing work in my workbook?

* Am I willing to enter into the group discussion—asking questions and expressing my personal opinions?

* Am I willing, if I think God is prodding me, to ask for personal ministry?

* Am I willing, if someone else expresses a need, to be used by God to speak today's truth into that person's life, just as Jesus spoke 2000 years ago?

If you answered "no" to any of these questions you may want to reconsider whether you should take this course. You are getting ready to touch the Word of God, and to examine the heart of God's truth. You should not enter into this course lightly or unadvisedly. Once you begin a serious study of the parables of Jesus, God, in all likelihood, will begin to teach you personally—about things in your life which need to be changed. If you are not ready for that to happen, you may want to sit this one out.

On the other hand, if you answered "yes" to the questions you are ready to proceed. Here are some immediate steps you can take to insure maximum benefit from the course.

1. Set Goals

This course is designed to help you understand not only the parables of Jesus, but the nature of God. It does not matter whether you are young or old, a seasoned Christian or just a seeker. God still speaks to anyone who will listen. Like the rain, which falls on the just and the unjust, God loves to reveal himself to all who reach out to Him. The principles learned over these next several class sessions will help you first of all to understand the parables of Jesus, but more important, begin to experience the truth He taught. Look ahead to what you need—and what kind of person you want to be. Do you want to be a better person? Do you want to think—and act—like Jesus? Set a goal and let this study help you get there.

2. Honestly Evaluate Your Present Condition

What are your needs—your real needs? A prisoner may feel his primary need is to be free. On the other hand, remember, Jesus said the greater bondage is the bondage of the soul and spirit. These parables will open the prison doors of your soul—allowing your spirit to soar free with joy and power.

Honestly evaluate your present condition as you begin this study of the parables, for without a willingness to face yourself it will be extremely difficult to understand what God is saying to you concerning your past, present and future.

Your faith commitment to dig into the Bible and examine the nature of God and his Kingdom must be accompanied by constant self-measurement and self-inventory. You know the kind of person you already are. You know the level of commitment you already display. You know your faith level. The question you must now face is "Am I willing to allow the awesome truth of these stories to change my life?"

At the end of each chapter there is a place where you—in the privacy of your own study—can evaluate your personal progress. The answers you give to the questions will give you some kind of spiritual indicator as to your progress week by week. The questions will also help fix the Word of God more firmly in your heart, and thus provide a reservoir of truth that the Holy Spirit can draw upon in the training and reshaping of your life until you are conformed to the image of Jesus.

3. You'll Not Pass This Way Again

Although God gives each man and woman infinite chances to improve and move into spiritual maturity, there are certain times when miracles are offered—and if refused—are not offered again. Thus, when discussion in class opens the door for you to express yourself, or ask for personal prayer, do not hesitate to respond. One of the things you will be doing during these sessions is learning to hear God—just as Jesus did.

When the disciples, having heard Jesus teach on the parable of the soils, pulled him aside and said "What did you mean?", he gave them direct answers.

When a religious scribe tried to trap Jesus over the question "Who is my neighbor?", Jesus told a story about a Samaritan who helped a wounded Jew. The story was so pointed the man was forced to make a choice: will I follow God, or will I refuse to follow Him?

Another time, after Peter had asked an honest question about the limits of forgiveness—"How many times shall I forgive someone who keeps sinning against me?"—Jesus told a story about forgiveness that shook Peter to his heels, and made him realize his entire approach was backwards.

In short, you'd better not ask God questions unless you're prepared to get straight, life-changing answers.

I urge you, therefore, to hear God—and do what He tells you to do, regardless of how illogical it may seem at the time. Only those who seek help find it. Only those who are open to truth receive it.

4. Study Each Chapter Before Class

Ideally, you should study each chapter in this workbook *before* coming to class. Look up each Scripture reference, answer all the questions by filling in the blanks and circling the true/false answers. Of course, if it is impossible to study ahead of time, you should still take part in the class activities.

5. Set Your Own Pace

One of the lessons you will learn as you study the Bible is this: God's patience is infinite as long as you are moving toward Him. The only time you will begin to feel pressure is when you close your mind, dig in your heels, or get off God's trail by pursuing false ideas and concepts. Do not be afraid to move slowly. To rush through this study may mean you learn all the right religious answers, but miss the Holy Spirit, Who is the one who brings miracles today. This course is designed to provoke you to do your own searching, thinking, and praying—and to demonstrate your faith in God.

6. Check Your Progress

Once you have completed the course, ask your chaplain, pastor, or group leader to sit down with you and review where you are in life. Remember the statement Jesus often made: "Those with ears to hear, let them hear."

7. Finally

Unless otherwise stated Scripture quotations are taken from the New International Version (NIV) of the Bible, copyright 1978 by New York International Bible Society and published by Zondervan Corporation, Grand Rapids, Michigan. Used by permission. Each chapter has a number of questions with accompanying Scripture references. By looking up the references you should be able to answer all the questions. Do not be afraid to fill in the blanks—even if you give the wrong answer. No one is going to grade you. This course is like those wonderful Special Olympics for handicapped children—everyone who enters is called a winner, regardless of how he finishes.

You will be awarded a Certificate of Completion at the end of the course, signed by me and your instructor. All you have to do is finish. That makes you a winner. By looking up the answers you will learn. Go ahead, try it. It's fun to learn—especially when you are learning about God.

As you study these parables of Jesus, hopefully you will begin to understand that He was not just telling stories, nor was He just talking to people back then. These stories—and their life-changing lessons—are for you today. Because we are constantly stumbling as we walk through this dark world, we need God to guide our footsteps, change our direction, and give us the ability to walk supernaturally.

Jesus, of course, had something far greater in mind than entertaining people with stories. In fact, His ultimate intention was to bring them to the place where they no longer had to be taught in parables, but could hear what God said through revelation knowledge. The day was coming, Jesus told his disciples, when "I shall no longer use this kind of language, but will tell you plainly about my Father" (John 16:25).

How would He then teach them? It would happen the way the prophet Jeremiah prophesied: His truth would be written on the hearts of men.

The purpose of this workbook, along with the accompanying video tape series, is to bring you to that place where the truth of God is written on your heart. And remember, the only thing more exciting than studying these wonderful stories of Jesus, is letting Him apply their truth to your life. Maybe you, too, will become a parable teller for others.

Jamie Buckingham

Lesson 1

The Parable of the Talents

Using Our Hidden Gifts

SCRIPTURE: Matthew 25:14-30
VIDEO REFERENCE: Lesson #1
SUPPLEMENTARY READING REFERENCE:
    Ten Parables of Jesus: Poking Holes in Religious Balloons
    Chapter I: "The Parable of the Talents"

1. The Purpose of the Parable

Jesus was approaching the end of His earthly ministry. For almost three years He had shared God's Word with the 12 men who had committed themselves to Him. They were His disciples—men He had called as the founders of His church. When He left, they would be responsible to put into practice and enlarge the work He had started.

They were to do more than maintain the very small teaching, preaching, and healing ministry Jesus had started, however.

What had Jesus commanded them to do with His message? (Mark 16:15)

_____

_____

_____

What method were they to use as they spread the Gospel? (I Corinthians 2:4)

_____

_____

Where did Jesus tell them to take the Gospel? (Acts 1:8)

1. _____

2. _____

3. _____

4. _____

There was a major problem, however. Jesus' disciples were all Jews. Jews, by their very nature, were protective of their race, their sacred writings, even their relationship with God. They saw themselves as a special race of people.

What had God done to make them special? (Deuteronomy 7:6)

_____

The Jews had not been chosen for themselves, however, God said they had been chosen to be a light.

To whom were the Jews to give the light? (Isaiah 42:6)

_____

Long after Jesus' death, Peter wrote a letter to some of his Christian friends outlining who they were in the light of the teaching of Moses.

Who did Peter say these Christian Jews were? (I Peter 2:9)

1. _____

2. _____

3. _____

4. _____

For what reason had they been chosen? (I Peter 2:9)

_____

_____

_____

_____

Protective of their heritage and defensive of their traditions, these Jews were afraid to open themselves to anyone except other Jews. The aim of the Scribes and Pharisees was to preserve the law, not share it.

They worked hard to keep the law exactly as it had been handed down by Moses on Mt. Sinai. In doing this, however, they had built a fence around their faith. It was impossible to keep all the laws. They had added to the law thousands of absurd and impossible requirements. They tightly held their scrolls, refusing to let the Gentiles read them, much less touch them. God, they believed, was for the Jews only.

Jesus knew it would be impossible for the disciples to carry on His ministry after He left if they did as the Scribes and Pharisees had done—simply hold on to that wonderful message, protecting it, preserving it, defending it.

The purpose of this parable, then, was to encourage His disciples to risk everything by giving His message away. It was not to be kept, preserved, defended—it was to be shared.

Jesus came to earth to make all things new. He had two basic reasons for coming. The first reason was to atone for the sins of all mankind by becoming the sacrificial lamb.

How did Jesus atone for our sins? (I Peter 2:24)

_____

_____

The second reason Jesus came to earth was to reveal the nature of God. He did this in a variety of ways.

How did Jesus reveal God's nature? (Check the correct answers.)

_____ Miracles

_____ Healings

_____ Teaching through parables

_____ His personal life style

_____ Forgiving sinners

_____ Confronting religious spirits

_____ Defining and pointing out sin

_____ Loving all people

_____ Laying down His life for mankind

List other ways you think Jesus revealed the nature of God.

_____

_____

_____

_____

_____

_____

Jesus challenged His disciples to enlarge and expand their concepts, their thoughts, their minds. He wanted them to take a different approach to God than the approach used by the Scribes and Pharisees, who had locked God into the past by their impossible rules, regulations, and traditions. The Scribes and Pharissees had paralyzed God's truth by hating anything new. Jesus wanted His disciples to venture out, explore, think new thoughts, and take great risks.

That was the purpose of this parable.

2. The Meaning of the Parable

This parable is one of several known as "the Olivet Discourses." Given just a few days before He was crucified, Jesus was teaching His disciples as they sat on the Mount of Olives overlooking the city of Jerusalem. It was important that they understand the nature of the Kingdom of Heaven (also known as the Kingdom of God) since they were to be the ones who would teach this to others.

To what did Jesus compare the Kingdom of Heaven? (Matthew 25:14)

_____

_____

How many major characters do we find in this parable? (Matthew 25:14-15)

_____ One

_____ Two

_____ Three

_____ Four

A talent was a sum of money, as a dollar, a peso, a pound, or a franc is a sum of money. In the days of Jesus, using our monetary standard, it would have been worth approximately $1,000.00.

Using this as a basic figure, how much money did the King give each of his servants before he left town? (Matthew 25:15)

Servant One $ _____

Servant Two $ _____

Servant Three $ _____

What did the King tell his servants to do with their money? (Matthew 25:14-15)

_____ To invest their money in stocks and bonds.

_____ To gamble it at the race track and make as much as they could.

_____ To put it in the bank and let it draw interest.

_____ To eat, drink, and be merry.

_____ To give it away to the poor.

_____ He didn't give them any instructions at all.

What did Servant One do with his money? (Matthew 25:16)

_____

Still using the dollar equivalent, how much money did he make by his investment, and how much did he wind up with when he was finished? (Matthew 25:16)

How much did he make? $ _____

How much did he wind up with? $ _____

What did Servant Two do with his money? (Matthew 25:17)

_____

Using the dollar equivalent, how much money did he make by his investment, and how much did he wind up with when he was finished? (Matthew 25:17)

How much did he make? $ _____

How much did he wind up with? $ _____

What did Servant Three do with his money? (Matthew 25:18)

_____

Using the dollar equivalent, how much money did he make by his investment, and how much did he wind up with when he was finished? (Matthew 25:18)

How much did he make? $ _____

How much did he wind up with? $ _____

This parable teaches, among other things, that for all things there is a day of reckoning. God holds each of us accountable, not only for what we receive, but for how we use it and why we act the way we do. In short, there is always a payday someday.

What becomes of the seed we sow? (Galatians 6:7)

_____

What do we reap if we sow to please our sinful nature? (Galatians 6:8)

_____

What do we reap if we sow to please the Spirit? (Galatians 6:8)

_____

How long was the King gone? (Matthew 25:19)

_____ Just a few days

_____ A long time

When the King returned and demanded an accounting all three servants came and stood before him. Servants One and Two told the King what they had done with his money. He was pleased and rewarded them.

In what three ways did he reward Servant One? (Matthew 25:21)

1. _____

2. _____

3. _____

In what three ways did he reward Servant Two? (Matthew 25:23)

1. _____

2. _____

3. _____

What excuse did Servant Three give for not increasing his money?
(Matthew 25:25)

_____ He didn't have time to get to the bank.

_____ He wasn't skilled in playing the stock market.

_____ His broker failed to return his phone calls.

_____ He wanted to invest in real estate but the king returned before he could close on a contract.

_____ He gave the money to the poor.

_____ His child was sick and he spent the money for medical bills.

_____ He was afraid; therefore he did nothing.

Decision-making is an important part of our Christian life. As stewards, we need to know what God wants us to do with our belongings.

What is the source of our guidance? (John 16:13)

_____

What does God say will happen to those who are self-seeking, who reject truth and follow evil? (Romans 2:8)

_____

What did the King do to Servant Three? (Matthew 25:30)

_____

What did the King do with Servant Three's $1,000.00? (Matthew 25:28)

_____

3. Lessons from the Parable

(1) The giving of spiritual gifts is a sovereign action.

Who gives spiritual gifts? (I Corinthians 12:6)

_____

(2) Everyone receives something from God.

Are there some who receive no spiritual gifts from God? (I Corinthians 12:7)

_____

List some of the gifts different people receive in order to serve God. (Romans 12:6-8)

1. _____

2. _____

3. _____

4. _____

5. _____

6. _____

7. _____

(3) God gives each of us differing gifts.

What does the King do equally with all his servants? (Matthew 25:19)

_____ Holds each fully accountable.

_____ Treats each differently according to circumstances.

_____ Gives an extension of time to work things out.

In the book of Luke, this same parable is told with a different twist. Luke recalls the King gave specific instructions before he left town.

What were these instructions? (Luke 19:13)

_____

_____

In Luke's account, the King received information that caused him to return home early.

What was this information? (Luke 19:14)

_____

_____

Do all receive the same gifts of the Holy Spirit? (I Corinthians 12:27-31)

_____ Yes

_____ No

(4) Some are more talented than others.

(5) If we faithfully use what we have, we receive more.

What did the King say about that? (Matthew 25:29)

_____

_____

The reward of work well done is not rest and a long vacation. God never allows us to sit back on our laurels as a reward for working hard. The fact we do work hard is an indication to God that He is able to trust us.

(6) What is the reward of work well done? (Matthew 25:21)

_____

(7) The call of God is always the call to risk what we have been given.

What was the king's reaction to Servant Three's charge that he was a hard man? (Matthew 25:26-27)

_____ Denied it.

_____ Said the servant had misjudged him.

_____ Agreed and said, "All the more reason..."

Which of these traits characterize Servant Three? (Matthew 25:24-27) (check correct answers.)

_____ Fear

_____ Unfaithfulness

_____ Complaining

_____ Obedience

_____ Wisdom

_____ Discerning nature

_____ Short-sightedness

(8) If we don't use what we have, we'll lose it.

What did Servant Three do with his money? (Matthew 25:25) (check correct answers)

_____ Squandered it in riotous living.

_____ Played 50—1 at the race track on a three-legged horse.

_____ Bet double or nothing on a pair of aces and lost to a full house.

_____ Invested it in a Jewish prayer shawl factory in Iran.

_____ Locked it in at five percent on a five-year CD the day before the prime rate soared to 14 percent.

_____ Hid the cash in the ground.

_____ None of the above.

What does this parable say to you? Check right answers, then add yours.

_____ Jesus will one day return and demand an accounting.

_____ We are all accountable for what we have even before He returns.

_____ All are equally accountable even though we do not have equal gifts.

_____

_____

_____

_____

WRAP UP

The precious gift of the Gospel has been given to us so we can share it with others. That is a tremendous risk, for it means we will be misunderstood, even persecuted. In fact, if we venture out and begin living for Jesus Christ we could lose everything. However, the Christian life is a life of adventure and faith. God never punishes anyone for trying and failing. He never condemns the person who loses because he risked too much. The only thing we have to fear is the result of doing nothing.

This fact is clear: We are not in charge of what we have. We will, however, be held accountable for all we've received. We do not make Christ King because we believe. He is King anyway—whether we obey or rebel—and He will, in the end, judge us all and hold us accountable, whether we've trusted Him or not.

FINAL LESSONS

1. The one question everyone has to answer is this: What did you do with the wonderful dreams and gifts God gave you?
2. "We live each day as if it were our last and each day as if there were a great future..." (Dietrich Bonhoeffer, written from a Nazi prison just a few days before he was executed.)

PERSONAL REVIEW QUESTIONS

Circle T (true) or F (false)

1. T F Risk should be part of the Christian life.

2. T F Jesus entrusted the Kingdom of God to human beings.

3. T F God gives everyone the same gifts and talents.

4. T F What matters most is the gift, not how we use it.

5. T F The reward of work well done is more work to do.

6. T F Fear is often the reason we are afraid to venture out for God.

7. T F The only way to keep a gift is to use it in the service of God.

8. T F Those who are highly talented are more blessed than those who have only a few talents.

9. T F The unfaithful servant was thinking only of his own security.

10. T F God does not punish us for trying, only for being afraid to try.

MEMORY VERSE

Matthew 25:23 (Memorize, then write it on these lines.)

_____

_____

_____

_____

TRUE OR FALSE ANSWERS:

1-T, 2-T, 3-F, 4-F, 5-T, 6-T, 7-T, 8-F, 9-T, 10-T

NOTES

Lesson 2

The Parable of the Unmerciful Servant

Forgiveness: The Only Way to Live

SCRIPTURE: Matthew 18:23-35
VIDEO REFERENCE: Lesson #2
SUPPLEMENTARY READING REFERENCE:
  Ten Parables of Jesus: Poking Holes in Religious Balloons
  Chapter II: "The Parable of the Unmerciful Servant"

1. Introduction

Parables are teaching stories based on fact. Jesus was a master storyteller, and the parables He told could have been fictional, or based on actual occurrences.

Jesus, however, had an anointed imagination. That's not so hard to understand when you remember He was Creator as well as Redeemer. He was with God in the creation process. When you are the Creator you can make up all kinds of things—including stories.

One of His deepest and most probing stories is this one, called the Parable of the Unmerciful Servant. It grew out of an extended conversation He had one day with His disciples.

They wanted to know who was the greatest person in the Kingdom of Heaven—no doubt thinking He might name one of them. After all, Simon Peter had just been part of one of the most significant miracles of all time. He had caught a fish in the Sea of Galilee on a hook and line that had in its mouth the exact amount of taxes owed by Jesus and His disciples.

Jesus surprised them all, however, by saying the greatest in the Kingdom of Heaven is a child. Then he warned them against offending the children and the childlike by causing them to sin.

He then told them what they were to do to keep from offending. They were to forgive those who sinned against them.

What is the three-fold step we are to take if someone sins against us? (Matthew 18:15-17)

1. _____
   _____

2. _____
   _____

3. _____
   _____

As far as we know Jesus only used the word "church" two times in His ministry. The first time He used it was when He said to Simon Peter, "Upon this rock I will build My church." In this passage He uses the word again, saying the final board of arbitration was the "church." It is important to keep in mind that the word "church" (actually the Greek word ecclesia) did not mean church as we know it today. In Jesus' day the "church" was the ruling council, or the elders, of the city. The church was the governing body. When Jesus told Peter, "Upon this rock I will build My church," He was talking about the government of God—not a building or an organization. The same applied when He said "the church" should arbitrate between disagreeing brothers. He was not talking about a congregational meeting. He was talking about the ruling, or governing body of the congregation.

The entire purpose of this three step procedure was to bring reconciliation between two people who disagreed. Jesus was talking about forgiveness.

That brought up the question which stimulated Jesus to tell this parable.

What was the question Peter asked? (Matthew 18:21)

_____

_____

How many times did Peter think he should forgive? (Matthew 18:21)

_____ Seven times

_____ Seventy-seven times

_____ Seven times seven

_____ Seven times seventy

_____ Seven times seventy-seven

_____ Seventy times seventy

How many times did Jesus say he should forgive? (Matthew 18:22)

_____ Seven times

_____ Seventy-seven times

_____ Seven times seven

_____ Seven times seventy

_____ Seven times seventy-seven

_____ Seventy-seven times seventy-seven

By His answer Jesus was outlining a principle, not a rule.

Did Jesus mean you should forgive 490 times, but on the 491st time the man sins against you you could take it out of his hide?

_____ Yes

_____ No

To understand the way of life Jesus was talking about we must understand the nature of God. God is love, the Bible says. Love means we not only forgive—we adopt forgiveness as a lifestyle. We are not allowed to add up merits and demerits. We forgive because God is love.

List fifteen characteristics of love. (I Corinthians 13:4-7)

1. _____
2. _____
3. _____
4. _____
5. _____
6. _____
7. _____
8. _____
9. _____
10. _____
11. _____
12. _____
13. _____
14. _____
15. _____

What did the Jewish law say you should do to the man who sinned against you? (Exodus 21:23-25)

If there was loss of life? _____

_____

If someone lost an eye in a fight? _____

_____

If someone knocked out someone's tooth? _____

_____

If a man lost his hand in a fight? _____

_____

If a man lost his foot in a fight? _____

_____

Jesus came to give new meaning to the Law. The Law, Jesus said, cannot be understood, much less kept, unless you understand why it was given. It was given to reveal God. The "eye for an eye" law was at heart a symbol of the fact that God cares about those who are wounded. He takes physical injury seriously.

The same is true with the "life for a life" law. While many use that Old Testament passage to justify capital punishment, they fail to realize that God loves human life and holds it sacred—even the life of a killer.

What did God have to say about capital punishment? (Ezekiel 33:11)

_____

_____

_____

Did Jesus come to abolish the Law? (Matthew 5:17)

_____ Yes

_____ No

What did Jesus come to do to the Law? (Matthew 5:17)

_____

In fulfilling the Law, Jesus gave new understanding to old meanings. He illustrates this by showing ways we can also fulfill the "eye for an eye" law.

If an evil person strikes us how should we respond? (Matthew 5:39)

_____

If someone sues you for your shirt off your back, what should you do? (Matthew 5:40)

_____

In Jesus' day, a Roman soldier would often conscript a Jewish man to carry his pack for him. By law the man had to carry the pack a mile. Then he was allowed to return to his work.

What did Jesus say you should do if forced to carry a pack for a mile? (Matthew 5:41)

_____

2. **The Meaning of the Parable**

The entire chapter of Matthew 18 deals with the subject of relationships— between people, between people and God. To illustrate all He had said, Jesus told this parable of the unmerciful servant.

Who are the three major characters in the story? (Matthew 18:23-32)

1. _____

2. _____

3. _____

Two of the characters have a similar problem—different only in size and scope.

What is the problem the men share? (Matthew 18:24, 28)

_____

What is the difference in the problem? (Matthew 18:24, 28)

_____

_____

_____

In Jesus' day a "talent" was worth about $1,000 in today's money. Servant One owed the master 10,000 talents—or the equivalent of $10 million. Servant Two, on the other hand, owed Servant One a much lesser sum. A denarius was worth about nine cents in today's money. That means he owed Servant One approximately $9.00.

Not considering the size of the debt each owed, what is similar between the two men? (Check right answers)

_____ Both are desperate because they are in debt.

_____ Both plead for forgiveness.

_____ Both have families.

_____ Both are capable of paying off the debt.

_____ Both could go to prison if they did not pay their debt.

_____ Both are servants of the same master.

_____ Both owe money to the same man.

To whom did the first man owe money? (Matthew 18:23-24)

_____

Both men were servants of the same master. Servant One owed the master directly. Servant Two was in debt to Servant One.

Since the master was master of both servants, when he forgave Servant One he was actually forgiving Servant Two, since the money owed to Servant One all belonged to the master.

What was the master's first intention with Servant One? (Matthew 18:25)

_____

_____

When Servant One begged for his life, what did the master do? (Matthew 18:27)

_____

_____

In the parable the man left the master's presence after being totally forgiven of a debt that amounted to a fortune so great it was impossible to repay.

How did Servant One respond to Servant Two's plea? (Matthew 18:28-30)

_____

_____

When the master heard of Servant One's unwillingness to forgive Servant Two, he took action.

How did the master react? (Matthew 18:32-34)

_____ He exacted harsh sentence immediately.

_____ He let the man off with a warning.

_____ He commended the man for being tough.

_____ He gave the man a third chance.

_____ He put him on probation.

_____ He allowed the man to plea bargain.

Did the two debtors ask to be forgiven, or ask for additional time, so they could honorably pay their debt? (Matthew 18:26, 29)

_____ Asked to be let off the hook.

_____ Pleaded for an extension so they could pay their bills.

There is a warning in this parable: A warning of love. It comes from the kindness of God's character. The warning is that those who have received God's love and forgiveness should let that love and forgiveness flow through them to others who have sinned against them.

What did Jesus say would happen if this was not done? (Matthew 6:15)

_____

_____

3. Judging Others

We cannot understand the forgiveness of God without understanding the justice of God. When you love much, it hurts to forgive. It's much easier to take revenge when you are sinned against than it is to forgive. Therefore, before we leave this lesson we need to take a brief look at judging others.

Does God judge us? (Psalm 96:13)

_____ Yes

_____ No

God is a God of justice. He calls on us to be like Him. That means we, too, are called upon to judge men. In Matthew 7 Jesus issues a warning about judging, however. Read the verses carefully, then answer carefully. The answer may not be as simple as it first seems.

Does Jesus tell us ever to judge one another? (Matthew 7:1-5)

_____ We are not to judge.

_____ It is right to judge.

_____ If we judge, we are to judge righteously—as God does.

Is the warning in Matthew 7:1 against all judging, or is it against judging with malice?

_____ Against all judging.

_____ Against judging with malice.

What does Jesus say we should do before we are qualified to judge? (Matthew 7:5)

_____

_____

By what standard should we judge one another? (Matthew 7:12)

_____

_____

What should be our attitude toward those who persecute us? (Matthew 5:44)

_____

In Jesus' story it is possible to see the master as a harsh, cruel overlord since in the end he winds up not only tossing a fellow into prison, but figuratively sending him to Hell. Many look on God that way, as a cruel God who sends people to Hell. However, as we read the entire story, not just the end, we see God as a different kind of God. While He did exact swift judgment, He had earlier exhibited that He was a forgiving God. Indeed, God did not send the man to Hell—the man, by his own actions, chose to go there.

How would you evaluate the God Jesus talked about in the parable? (check right answers)

_____ Merciful

_____ Forgiving

_____ Just

_____ Generous

What happens when we forgive those who sin against us? (Matthew 6:14)

_____

What happens when we refuse to forgive those who sin against us? (Matthew 6:15)

_____

How are we to treat one another? (I John 4:7-8)

_____

WRAP UP

God is a loving, but just God. He expects of His followers the same as He gives to us. As He forgives us, so He expects us to forgive others. We owed a debt we could not pay. Jesus paid a debt He did not owe. Now it is up to us to forgive one another since we have been forgiven. As we forgive each other, so we show God our appreciation for what He has done for us. The greatest gift we can bestow on God is the gift of treating others the way He treated us. The greatest debt we owe is the imperative that we do not forget His forgiveness to us.

FINAL LESSON

Do unto others as you would have them do unto you.

PERSONAL REVIEW QUESTIONS

Circle T (true) or F (false)

1. T F This parable teaches it's okay to pile up a big debt and not pay.

2. T F If someone has sinned against us we should take them before the church as soon as possible.

3. T F Judging is okay if we have a right spirit.

4. T F Even Jesus had a limit on how many times He forgave.

5. T F If you forgive seventy times seven and the man keeps on sinning against you, you should break his thumbs to teach him a lesson.

6. T F We should forgive because God has forgiven us.

7. T F Holding grudges could get us into trouble with God.

8. T F We should do unto others what they do unto us.

9. T F Personal revenge is sometimes justified in God's eyes.

10. T F It is always better to forgive than take vengence.

11. T F God said it is always easier to forgive than to take revenge.

12. T F Jesus forgave those who unjustly executed Him.

MEMORY VERSE

Matthew 5:44 (Memorize, then write it on these lines.)

_____

_____

_____

TRUE OR FALSE ANSWERS:

1-F, 2-F, 3-T, 4-F, 5-F, 6-T, 7-T, 8-F, 9-F, 10-T, 11-F, 12-T

NOTES

Lesson 3
The Parable of the Two Houses
High Living in Tough Places

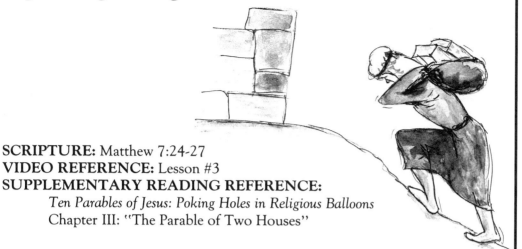

SCRIPTURE: Matthew 7:24-27
VIDEO REFERENCE: Lesson #3
SUPPLEMENTARY READING REFERENCE:
 Ten Parables of Jesus: Poking Holes in Religious Balloons
 Chapter III: "The Parable of Two Houses"

1. Introduction

The most famous sermon ever preached is called the Sermon on the Mount. It is found in Matthew 5-7. Most Bible scholars agree, however, that the content of the sermon is a compilation of a number of Jesus' teachings, gathered together by the Gospel writers into one discourse. Most of the teachings in Matthew also appear in Luke, but are not in the same order—nor even all together. This is additional evidence that the sermon is really the gathering of a number of Jesus' short teachings.

The sermon in Matthew begins with groups of proverbs, called Beatitudes. These are followed by several small parables about salt and lamps. Then Jesus takes a number of Old Testament teachings and elaborates on them—giving not only the words but the meaning and the intent.

He says, for instance, that while the law says you should not kill, the intent of God is that you should not hate. In fact, you ought to love other people as you love yourself—doing unto others as you would have them do unto you.

The Scribes and Pharisees were bent out of shape over the meaning of adultery, Jesus told His disciples. But the question is not really what you do with your body—the problem is in your heart. Do you lust? Do you covet someone else's spouse? Jesus never condoned sexual looseness. Instead, He asked His followers to understand why the law forbidding it had been written in the first place. God wanted men and women to live together in faithfulness in marriage, with hearts so pure toward God that they would desire only their marriage partners.

Jesus closed out these teachings with a simple parable of two houses—one built on rock and the other on sand.

To whom was the Sermon on the Mount preached? (Matthew 5:1-2)

_____ To the multitudes

_____ To Jesus' disciples

In the sermon Jesus listed eight types of people who are "blessed," or "happy." **List the people who are blessed.** (Matthew 5:3-11)

1. _____

2. _____

3. _____

4. _____

5. _____

6. _____

7. _____

8. _____

2. The Parable

At the close of this famous "sermon" Jesus tells this simple parable and addresses two groups of people.

Who are the two groups—actually two men—Jesus refers to? (Matthew 7:24, 26)

1. _____

2. _____

What does the wise man do besides hearing Jesus' teaching? (Matthew 7:24)

_____

What does the foolish man do with Jesus' teaching? (Matthew 7:26)

_____

How many houses appear in Jesus parable? (Matthew 7:24, 26)

_____ One house with two different builders.

_____ Two houses with the same builder.

_____ Two houses with two builders.

In Israel there are a number of dry riverbeds called wadis. These wadis, or "washes" as they are known in the American Southwest, are often deep canyons with steep sides and sandy bottoms. Israel is a dry, arid land. Crisscrossing the nation are these wadis which run essentially toward the Mediterranean Sea to the west, or to the Jordan River and the Dead Sea on the east. They stay dry most of the year. But when it rains in the highlands, the water cascades down off the desert mountains, running in torrents over the hard, alkaline soil which absorbs very little, and eventually spill into the wadis. Almost instantly what was a dry, sandy canyon becomes a raging river. Everything in front of the rush is swept away. Destroyed.

Who is the central figure in each story? (Matthew 7:24, 26)

_____

Where did the wise man build his house? (Matthew 7:24)

_____

Where did the foolish man build his house? (Matthew 7:26)

_____

The same thing happened to both houses.

What happened to both the house on the rock and the house on the sand? (Matthew 7:24, 26) (check correct answers)

_____ Rain fell on both houses.

_____ Wind blew on both houses.

_____ Both houses were caught in a flood.

_____ Both houses were built by the same builder.

_____ Both houses had tin roofs.

_____ Both houses were swept away in the flood.

_____ Both houses developed cracks in the foundation.

_____ Both houses had back yard swimming pools.

In the Bible, rain is usually seen as a sign of blessing. However, in Jesus' parable the rain creates a disaster because the contractor did not build correctly. What is blessing to one man may be a curse to another if the foundation is not correct.

What is the solid foundation? (Matthew 7:24)

_____

Great debates rage as to why good people suffer and why evil people prosper. These are addressed, to some degree, by the book of Job as well as by other Scripture passages, such as Psalm 73 and Isaiah 53.

Upon whom does the rain (the blessing) of God fall? (Matthew 5:45)

_____

According to Jesus' parable everyone builds some kind of house. In the Kingdom of God there are no renters, no sidewalk people. Everyone puts down some sort of foundation. The house represents our character, our lifestyle, our goals, our dreams, our behavior. There is no way to be non-decisive about our life's house.

What did Jesus say about those who believe? (John 3:18)

_____

What did Jesus say about those who believe not? (John 3:18)

_____

What will every house have to face? (Matthew 7:25,27)

_____

_____

The Bible teaches that there are "ideal conditions." Rains, winds, floods—all are a part of life. In another parable the farmer rejects his worker's request for ideal growing conditions.

What did the farmer tell his workers? (Matthew 13:24-30)

_____

_____

_____

There are a number of "constants" in Jesus' story: The house builder, the rain, the wind, the floods.

What is the one variable? (Matthew 7:25-27)

_____

The Scribes—those teachers who had memorized the law of Moses as well as the huge books of interpretations of that law called the Talmud—taught by quoting the old rabbis. If the rabbi had said it, it could be true. If several rabbis had said it, it must be true. Jesus, however, used a different method of teaching. In fact, He never quoted a single rabbi.

What was different between Jesus' teachings and those of the Scribes? (Matthew 7:28-29)

_____

_____

Jesus never claimed to have authority. He just showed it in His actions and teachings. (Matthew 7:28)

_____ True

_____ False

Where did Jesus' authority come from? (John 5:26-27)

_____

Jesus said the wise man was the man who listened to His sayings then built his life principles upon them. He likened this to a builder who builds his house on solid rock.

Paraphrase seven of the "sayings" of Jesus we should be using for foundation stones in our lives.

1. (Matthew 6:1-4) _____

_____

_____

_____

2. (Matthew 5:5-8) _____

_____

_____

_____

3. (Matthew 7:1-5) _____

_____

_____

_____

4. (Matthew 7:21-23) _____

_____

_____

_____

_____

5. (Matthew 6:14-15) _____

_____

_____

_____

6. (Matthew 6:19-22) _____

_____

_____

_____

7. (Matthew 5:33-37) _____

_____

_____

_____

What do we generally call the prayer Jesus taught His disciples to pray? (Matthew 6:9-13)

_____

3. Bible Foundations

There are many Bible references to the solid rock foundation.

Who is our rock? (Psalm 18:2, Psalm 92:15)

_____

Foundations on rock are never in the low places. They are always found in the high places, far above the floor of the wadi. That means we have to stretch to reach the place where we are to build.

How high is the rock upon which we build? (Psalm 61:2)

_____

Who is the rock of our refuge? (Psalm 71:3)

_____

Where were our feet before they were set on the rock of Jesus? (Psalm 40:2)

_____

After Simon Peter received direct knowledge from God that Jesus was "the Christ, the Son of the Living God," Jesus told him the foundation of the church would be built on that ability to hear God.

Where did Jesus say He would build His church? (Matthew 16:18)

_____

What does Paul call Jesus? (I Corinthians 10:4)

_____

WRAP UP

The teachings of Jesus are the foundation of the world. Any life, any institution, any dream, any nation built on any other foundation except the teachings of Jesus Christ will fail. We have a choice of building on the high, difficult solid rock of the teachings of Jesus, or in the low, easy place in the sand of our own desires and intellect. However, when the storms come—and they will come—only the house on the solid foundation will stand. All the rest will fall and great disaster will follow.

FINAL LESSON

The only foundation which will not be shaken is the solid rock of Jesus Christ. A life committed to Him, while constantly under assault, will never fall.

PERSONAL REVIEW QUESTIONS

Circle T (true) of F (false)

1. T   F   Jesus preached His Sermon on the Mount to the multitudes.

2. T   F   Jesus preached His Sermon on the Mount to the disciples.

3. T   F   The parable of the two houses refers to Middle Eastern architecture only.

4. T   F   It's okay to build on sand (disobey the teachings of Jesus) if your children are grown and your wife agrees.

5. T   F   Hard times never come to people who build on rock.

6. T   F   Foolish people think they can cheat on God's way and get away with it.

7. T   F   Even though the floods and wind may come, if a person has built on Jesus he'll not fall.

8. T   F   Jesus was recognized as a teacher with spiritual authority.

9. T   F   Jesus told His parable to stress the importance of obeying His teachings.

10. T   F   The central figure in each story is the house builder.

11. T   F   The parable indicates each man has freedom of choice.

12. T   F   Jesus is the only foundation upon which we should build our lives.

MEMORY VERSE

Matthew 16:16 (Memorize, then write it on these lines.)

_____

_____

_____

_____

_____

TRUE OR FALSE ANSWERS:

1-F, 2-T, 3-F, 4-F, 5-F, 6-T, 7-T, 8-T, 9-T, 10-T, 11-T, 12-T

NOTES

39

NOTES

Lesson 4

The Parable of the Five Foolish Maidens

Reserve Strength for Tough Times

SCRIPTURE: Matthew 25:1-13
VIDEO REFERENCE: Lesson #4
SUPPLEMENTARY READING REFERENCE:
    Ten Parables of Jesus: Poking Holes in Religious Balloons
    Chapter IV: "The Parable of the Five Foolish Maidens"

1. Introduction

It was the last week of Jesus' life on earth. He was in Jerusalem. Jesus was giving His disciples a cram lesson on the nature of the Kingdom of God—the kingdom they (and we) would be responsible for until He returned. Seated in the courtyard of a Jerusalem house located on the Mount of Olives, He told the first of two stories which illustrated important things He wanted His disciples to remember. The second story, which we studied in Lesson One, was about a man who was getting ready to go on a long journey and gave three of his trusted servants unequal amounts of money to invest while he was gone. It is called the parable of the talents.

The other story had to do with a group of bridesmaids waiting for the groom to appear for his wedding. Five of these bridesmaids were wise; five were foolish.

Jesus had just finished telling His disciples that certain signs would accompany the "end times." While Jesus may have been talking about the events which would precede the end of the world just prior to His Second Coming, it is obvious He was also talking about the fall of Jerusalem which took place in 70 AD. At that time the end of the world as the Jews knew it would come to pass as the nation of Israel would be utterly destroyed. The Jews, especially the followers of Jesus, would be scattered to the far corners of the earth when similar things would take place as those preceding the end of the world. He began by warning them to watch out for certain things which could deceive them.

What were the disciples to watch out for? (Matthew 24:5)

False teachers

Before the "end" comes, what should we expect to hear? (Matthew 24:6)

_____

What three things will precede the end of peaceful times? (Matthew 24:7)

1. _____

2. _____

3. _____

How did Jesus describe these signs? (Matthew 24:8)

_____

As the end approaches Jesus warned His disciples that there would be persecution and that the followers of Jesus would be hated by all nations and put to death. This would fulfill a prophecy spoken by Daniel.

What was the prophecy given by Daniel which was literally fulfilled in 70 AD when the Romans destroyed Jerusalem and scattered the Jews over all the earth? (Daniel 11:31)

_____

_____

He told them not to be discouraged when certain things happened among the believers.

What did He say to expect? (Matthew 24:10-12)

1. _____

_____

_____

2. _____

_____

3. _____

_____

This was followed by a promise that those who are loyal to Jesus would be saved, and the Gospel would be preached in the whole world before the end comes. Then, obviously referring to the end of the world, Jesus warned His disciples to remain faithful and wise—telling them a little parable about a wise servant who had been put in charge of the servants in his household awaiting the coming of the King. Such a servant was to remain in a state of readiness.

When did Jesus say He would come again? (Matthew 24:44, 50)

_____

_____

Jesus then proceeded to tell this story of the wedding banquet attended by five foolish bridesmaids and five wise bridesmaids.

2. The Wedding Party

To illustrate the end times Jesus told the story of a wedding party. The Jews' wedding feast lasted seven days. It began with a reception, usually in the home of the bride's father. This was followed by a feast, called the "wedding supper" when the bridegroom appeared. It was often something of a game to guess just when the bridegroom might appear.

Remember, the story was told to Jesus' disciples. It does not have to do with people who are lost and people who are saved. It was a warning to those in the kingdom, who were awaiting his coming, to remain in a state of preparedness.

He likens His Second Coming to the coming of the bridegroom to be with his bride—the church.

What did the ten bridesmaids do when they thought the bridegroom was coming? (Matthew 25:1)

_____

_____

How did Jesus describe these young women? (Matthew 25:2)

_____

_____

Why did he call five of the bridesmaids "foolish"? (Matthew 25:3)

_____

_____

Why were the other five bridesmaids described as "wise"? (Matthew 25:4)

_____

_____

Jesus is saying the person who does not plan ahead, who does not have reserves for tough times, is a fool.

3. The Description of a Fool

The Bible does not equate foolishness with lack of intelligence. A fool, in the Biblical sense, is a person with great intelligence who does not use his intelligence wisely.

Who is the greatest fool of all? (Psalm 14:1)

one who says "there is no God"!

Wisdom begins by fearing God, Solomon said.

What do fools do? (Proverbs 1:7)

despise wisdom + dicipline

What do fools hate? (Proverbs 1:22)

Knowledge

What do fools make fun of? (Proverbs 14:9)

Jesus described the man who built his house on sand rather than a solid rock foundation as a fool.

What did Jesus say the wise man did with Jesus' teachings? (Matthew 7:24)

In another parable Jesus called a man a fool for not planning for the future.

What did the rich man do which classified him as a fool? (Luke 12:18-19)

3. The Ten Bridesmaids

The bridesmaids had actually gone out to greet the groom and escort him back into the house. Their purpose was to stand along the road with their lamps to light the way for him. When the bridegroom did not show up for a long time, the bridesmaids grew sleepy.

Did Jesus call them foolish for dropping off to sleep? (Matthew 25:5)

_____ Yes

_____ No

When did the bridegroom show up? (Matthew 25:6)

_____

Will Jesus, who is represented by the bridegroom, let us know before He comes again so we can get ready? (Matthew 24:44)

_____ Yes

_____ No

The little, hand-held lamps were filled with olive oil. Each had a wick. When the bridesmaids went to sleep their lamps had just about burned out. When they awoke to the announcement that the bridegroom was actually on his way, they all started getting ready.

What did all ten girls do? (Matthew 25:7)

_____

Doubtlessly the foolish girls had made fun of the other five bridesmaids for bringing with them extra oil. It was inconvenient to bring along reserves. But the wise girls knew there was no guarantee when the bridegroom would show up. So they came prepared.

What did the foolish girls do when they realized they didn't have oil for their lamps? (Matthew 25:8)

_____

Why did the wise girls refuse to share? (Matthew 25:9)

_____

What did they tell the foolish girls to do? (Matthew 25:9)

_____

What happened while the foolish girls were out buying more oil? (Matthew 25:10-12)

_____

_____

_____

_____

_____

It is not enough to know and love Jesus. We must be filled with His Spirit.

What can happen to those who love Jesus but do not have adequate spiritual reserves? (Matthew 24:12)

_____

How did Jesus say we should await His coming? (Luke 12:35)

_____

_____

How does Jesus want to find us when He returns? (Luke 12:38)

_____

If you are filled with the Spirit you will always have a reservoir within you.

What did Jesus say would happen to the person who is filled with His Spirit? (John 7:38)

_____

_____

_____

How can we be filled with the Spirit of Jesus and so have adequate reserves when tough times come? (Luke 11:13)

_____

_____

WRAP UP

Everyone who has accepted Jesus has oil in his lamp. The wise man, however, realizing that tough times may come before Jesus returns, always plans ahead. He does this by asking God to fill him with the Holy Spirit so that He has reserve spiritual power. The question this parable asks is this: Do I have spiritual reserves? What will happen to me when crisis comes? Have I fortified myself with God's Spirit so I will be able to stand and not fall?

FINAL LESSON

No one knows the time of Christ's return. The foolish person lives for today only. The wise person plans ahead.

PERSONAL REVIEW QUESTIONS

Circle T (true) or F (false)

1. T F The wise man prepares for the future by asking God to fill Him with his Holy Spirit.

2. T F The bridegroom is too loving to lock the door on anyone.

3. T F If we study the Scriptures we can tell just when Christ will return.

4. T F Even though tough times may come, if we believe it means we are automatically prepared.

5. T F Jesus is saying that while your lamp may burn out, as long as you have a reserve supply you'll be okay.

6. T F God does not hold us accountable for the future, only for the present and past.

7. T F The wise person always has a reserve supply.

8. T F I can depend on my friends to help me if I run low on spiritual power.

9. T F Each of us is accountable for our own salvation.

10. T F It's not my fault if I run out of spiritual power.

MEMORY VERSE

Luke 12:40 (Memorize, then write it on these lines.)

_____

_____

_____

_____

TRUE OR FALSE ANSWERS:

1-T, 2-F, 3-F, 4-F, 5-T, 6-F, 7-T 8-F, 9-T, 10-F

NOTES

Lesson 5

The Parable of the Good Shepherd

God Loves Black Sheep—Especially

SCRIPTURE: Luke 15:3-7
VIDEO REFERENCE: Lesson #5
SUPPLEMENTARY READING REFERENCE:
    Ten Parables of Jesus: Poking Holes in Religious Balloons
    Chapter V: "The Parable of the Good Shepherd"

1. Introduction

This is one of three stories Jesus told, back to back, to show His critics that God is a God of love. The Pharisees genuinely thought God loved only good people—those who kept the law. Trying to convince people that God loves folks when they believe God is a cop or a prison warden— is a tough procedure.

A lot of people don't understand fatherhood. Their own fathers were cruel, didn't care, were absent when they needed them, or never did exist. Tell someone like this that God is father, and all they can picture is their own father. If God is like that, forget it!

Therefore Jesus not only talked about God as a father, He illustrated God in other ways. Primarily He was trying to show people that God loved. Especially does God love those who have a great need for love: the lost, the frightened, the soiled, the losers, and failures of this world. To get that point over Jesus told three stories about lostness.

What were the three things which were lost in Jesus' stories? (Luke 15:4, 8, 11-13).

1. _____

2. _____

3. _____

Jesus' story of the lost sheep grew out of the stress created by the presence of "sinners" at Jesus' dinner table. The Pharisees were offended. "What right do you, a rabbi, have to eat with sinners?" the Scribes and Pharisees challenged Jesus. "If God hates sinners, you should hate them, too."

But they had their basic premise wrong. God does hate sin, but that's not the way He feels about sinners.

What does God want to do about sinners? (I Timothy 1:15)

_____

How many people in the world are "sinners"? (Romans 3:23)

_____

How does God want us to feel about evil? (Amos 5:15)

_____

Those who love the Lord should do what when it comes to evil? (Psalm 97:10)

_____

If God hates sin but loves sinners, how should we treat those who commit evil and hate us? (Romans 12:14)

_____

The Scribes and Pharisees did not believe God loved sinners. To try to illustrate who God really is, Jesus told the story of a lost sheep—and the reaction of the good shepherd.

As with most of Jesus' parables, he probably began His story by pointing at a nearby field where a flock of sheep were returning to the fold for the night. They had been out on the hillside all day, grazing. It was now close to sundown and the weary shepherd was bringing them in. His sheepdog was running around the sheep, forcing the strays back into the flock.

This was a familiar sight in Jesus' day. Many of the people were farmers and shepherds. Sheep were a valuable commodity. Every Jew had heard the heroic stories of David, the shepherd, who had often risked his life by battling wild animals which attacked his father's sheep.

The Old Testament Scriptures were filled with refrences to sheep and shepherds. The most famous Psalm began with the words: "The Lord is my shepherd." The prophet Ezekiel spoke of good sheperds and false sheperds, and severely warned against those who used the sheep for their own purposes. Thus, Jesus' story about the shepherd and his sheep was in a familiar setting.

2. The Setting

Why did Jesus tell this story? (Luke 15:1-3)

_____

_____

_____

_____

What were the two groups of people who were listening to Jesus' parable? (Luke 15:1)

1. _____

2. _____

The Pharisees viewed God as a lawmaker, a policeman (an enforcer of the law), and a judge.

How did Jesus address God? (Matthew 6:9)

_____

What was it the Pharisees didn't like about Jesus? (Luke 15:2)

_____

3. The Sheep

In this story where did the shepherd first notice there was a problem? (Luke 15:4)

_____ While he was tending his sheep in the open country.

_____ After he got back to the sheepfold at night.

_____ On the way home from the pasture.

How does Jesus begin His story? (Luke 15:4)

_____ With a strong accusation.

_____ With a disturbing question.

_____ With a denunciation of wandering sheep.

How many sheep were in the original flock? (Luke 15:4)

_____ 40

_____ 100

_____ 99

_____ 144,000

How do you think Jesus' listeners would naturally answer the question as to whether the shepherd would leave the sheep to seek the stray?

_____ Yes, I would go right away.

_____ Not me.

A number of things could have happened to the stray sheep. The sheep could have been lost because of illness. It may have developed a disease and dropped by the path. To have brought it home could infect the other sheep.

It may have become disoriented and simply wandered off into the desert. To have located it at night would have been virtually impossible.

It may have fallen off a cliff and be dead. There was no need to go back.

It may have been bitten by a poisonous snake and be dying. Even though the sheep was still alive, there was nothing that could be done to save its life.

It may have been in rebellion against the shepherd, wandering away in search of greener grass because it disagreed with the shepherd's choice of pasture. Perhaps the sheep needed to be taught a lesson by leaving it out all night.

It may have been killed by a wolf or mountain lion. To go back and try to find it might disturb the wild animal, causing it to attack the shepherd.

Where do you think the lost sheep was? (Check areas where it could have been.)

_____ In a deep canyon

_____ In another shepherd's fold.

_____ Lost in the wilderness.

_____ Sodom and Gomorrah.

_____ Caught on a high ledge.

_____ It left early and was safe at home.

All God's sheep are easily identified. (John 10:16)

_____ True

_____ False

4. The Good Shepherd

Who does the good shepherd represent in Jesus' story?

_____ The Heavenly Father.

_____ Jesus.

_____ Any follower of God.

_____ All of the above.

Who did Jesus say needed a physician? (Matthew 9:12)

_____

Who did Jesus say He had come to invite into the kingdom? (Matthew 9:13)

_____

For whom did Christ die? (Romans 5:8)

_____

Since God loves sinners it's okay for us to continue in sin. (Romans 6:1-2)

_____ True

_____ False

Who did God love enough to send His son to die for? (John 3:16)

_____

Did God send His son to condemn us of our sins or to save us from our sins? (John 3:17)

_____ Condemn

_____ Save

What must a person do to have eternal life? (John 3:16)

_____

Who would be placed in danger if the shepherd were to go back and try to find the lost sheep? (Luke 15:4)

_____ The shepherd.

_____ The remaining sheep.

_____ The people in the village.

In Jesus' parable he tells the story of a shepherd who went out, found his lost sheep, and returned him to the fold.

What did the shepherd expect the villagers to do when they saw him coming home with the lost sheep? (Luke 15:6)

_____ Complain that the shepherd was late for dinner.

_____ Get angry that he had left the 99.

_____ Gripe that the shepherd spent time looking for a single stray.

_____ Rejoice.

What does the good shepherd do for his sheep? (John 10:15)

_____

_____

How does the good shepherd know which sheep belong to him? (John 10:27)

_____

_____

What does the good shepherd give his sheep? (John 10:28)

_____

_____

5. **The False Shepherd**

Shepherds are mentioned throughout the Bible. Many of the ancient Bible heroes were shepherds. Abraham, Isaac, and Jacob (later called Israel) were all shepherds. David was a shepherd before he became king. Jesus called himself "the good shepherd." But the Bible also has much to say about false shepherds.

What did God say would happen to false shepherds? (Ezekiel 34:10)

_____

_____

What should a good shepherd do? (Ezekiel 34:2)

_____

List 10 marks of a false shepherd. (Ezekiel 34:3-4)

1. _____

2. _____

3. _____

4. _____

5. _____

6. _____

7. _____

8. _____

9. _____

10. _____

What happens to sheep with a poor or false shepherd? (Ezekiel 34:5)

1. _____

2. _____

How do sheep know which shepherd to follow? (John 10:27)

_____

Who does God say the sheep belong to? (Ezekiel 34:6,8)

_____

6. A New Vision of God

God, Jesus says, is a God of love. In this parable we see four aspects of that love.

1. The love of God is an individual love. He loves each of us personally— not for what we've done, but for who we are.

2. The Love of God is a patient love. God is never in a hurry.

3. The love of God is a seeking love. God is not only out searching for those who are lost, he wants us to be searchers, too.

4. The love of God is a rejoicing love. Instead of being irritated when someone we think needs to be punished receives Christ and is saved, we should rejoice.

How did the father react in Jesus' parable of the prodigal son when his lost son came home? (Luke 15:23)

_____

How did the woman react in Jesus parable of the lost coin when she found what she had lost? (Luke 15:9)

_____

How does God react when an evil person repents and turns to God? (Luke 15:7,10)

_____

WRAP UP

God rejoices when the lost is found. He never hits us with moral lectures. He never condemns us for what we have done. He receives us, brings us to his home, and gives us His nature and power.

FINAL LESSON

God is genuinely drawn and attracted to the irreligious. He loves the black sheep of the human race: the rebels, the sinners, the angry, those who are out-of-control. He sees in them something nobody else seems to be able to see. The rough, the profane, the fallen, the thieves, the immoral, the earthy, those of turbulent passions—He loves them all.

Oh, what they become when Jesus finds them and brings them home.

PERSONAL REVIEW QUESTIONS

Circle T (true) or F (false)

1. T   F   Like most of Jesus' parables, this story was told to correct wrong thinking.

2. T   F   Both the Pharisees and "sinners" were listening as Jesus spoke.

3. T   F   Jesus told the story to reveal the nature of God.

4. T   F   The good shepherd expected his neighbors to rejoice that the lost sheep had been found.

5. T   F   The good shepherd sent the assistant shepherd to find the lost sheep.

6. T   F   The lost sheep probably would have found its way home anyway.

7. T   F   Jesus says we should rejoice when "sinners" are interested in the Gospel message.

8. T   F   Sinners need to straighten up their act before they can expect the shepherd to come after them.

9. T   F   God is hard on false shepherds who don't love all the sheep.

10. T   F   God loves to kill guilty people.

11. T   F   God says he rejoices when guilty people repent.

12. T   F   God prefers to give us a sentence to life rather than a death sentence.

13. T   F   Jesus came to invite the lost to join his church.

14. T   F   If you are bad, God won't love you until you repent.

15. T   F   God loves angry rebels as much as those who willingly submit.

16. T   F   Since God loves rebels, we should rebel even more so we can experience even more of God's love.

MEMORY VERSE

Luke 15:7 (Memorize, then write it on these lines)

_____

_____

_____

_____

TRUE OR FALSE ANSWERS:

1-T, 2-T, 3-T, 4-T, 5-F, 6-F, 7-T, 8-F, 9-T, 10-F, 11-T, 12-T, 13-T, 14-F, 15-T, 16-F

NOTES

Lesson 6

The Parable of the Sower and the Seed
Getting Ready for Better Things

SCRIPTURE: Matthew 13:1-23 (Also Mark 4:1-20; Luke 8:4-15)
VIDEO REFERENCE: Lesson #6
SUPPLEMENTARY READING REFERENCE:
   Ten Parables of Jesus: Poking Holes in Religious Balloons
   Chapter VI: "The Parable of the Sower and the Seed"

1. Introduction

There are eight parables found in Matthew 13. All share the same theme: the kingdom of heaven (also called the kingdom of God). These "kingdom parables" are different, however, in that they stress various aspects of God's kingdom. Some focus on the King. Others concentrate on the subjects of the King. Still others accent the kingdom's realm, or character. Others blend each of these elements together.

Many people in Jesus' day were looking for a Messiah who would establish an earthly kingdom—one that would drive away the hated Romans and establish Judaism in its rightful place as the government of the world.

Those who accepted Jesus as the Messiah hoped that's what He would do. Even though they loved Him for His character and respected Him for His miracles, most were disappointed in His continuous emphasis on a "kingdom within" rather than an earthly kingdom.

The parables found in Matthew 13 show how the kingdom was (and is) to enter and spread throughout the entire world first. Only then would come the final climax.

This parable is the most revealing of all Jesus' parables with regard to how the Kingdom will shape up, who will oppose it, how some people will enter presumptuously and then fall away, and others will remain and bear fruit. This parable will give you a firm understanding of what to expect as the Gospel takes root in your own life.

The parable comes from the world of farming. All of Jesus' parables had some common point of interest the people could identify. He told stories about sheep and shepherds, houses on sand and rock, vineyards and landowners. This story was about a farmer. But it was also about his seed. Most of all, it was about the soil.

Picture Jesus sitting with His disciples around Him and a much larger crowd behind them. He points to a nearby field where a farmer is walking the furrows, sowing seed in newly plowed ground. Then He tells His parable.

2. The Word of God

This parable is different in that it includes a complete explanation of the parable.

What does the seed represent? (Mark 4:14)

_____

Where should the Word of God take root? (Deuteronomy 6:6)

_____

When Jesus was tempted by Satan in the wilderness, Satan wanted Him to turn stones into bread in order to feed the hungry. Jesus replied with a scripture reference from Deuteronomy in which He said man had other needs beside bread.

What does man need to live on besides bread? (Matthew 4:4, Dueteronomy 8:3)

_____

_____

The Word of God is far more than the Bible. While the Bible contains the words of God, and is holy and sacred in that it is a true and accurate record of what God spoke and has accomplished in history, John says the Word of God is much bigger than the Bible.

Who is the Word of God? (John 1:1-2, 14)

_____

What does the Word of God (Jesus) bring? (John 1:17)

1. _____

2. _____

How long will God's Word be around? (Isaiah 40:8, I Peter 1:25)

_____

What did Jesus say would pass away before His Words passed away?
(Mark 13:31)

_____

While this is essentially a parable of the soils, it is also a parable of the seed—God's Word. As we read the parable we find the seed does not always take root. There are a number of different reasons for this. But it is important to remember that while the soil may fail, the seed is still good seed, and even if it does not take root in our heart for the reasons listed in the parable, it will still take root someplace.

What can we expect of God's Word? (Isaiah 55:10-11)

_____

_____

_____

Why is Scripture given to us? (II Timothy 3:16)

1. _____

2. _____

3. _____

4. _____

3. **The Hard Heart**

Some of the seed fell on the hardened path where the farmer walked.

What happened to that seed? (Matthew 13:4)

_____

Who do the birds in Jesus' parable represent? (Matthew 13:19)

_____ The Pharisees

_____ Traditions held by the Scribes

_____ The Romans

_____ The devil

Unless seed is covered by earth it will not sprout. This seed lays on top of the ground. It might be that later someone would come along with a plow and turn the earth over, giving the seed a chance to sprout.

How soon did Satan act when the seed fell on hard ground? (Mark 4:15)

_____

Name five reasons you think men harden their hearts, causing them to reject God's truth.

1. _____

   _____

2. _____

   _____

3. _____

   _____

4. _____

   _____

5. _____

   _____

The first thing Satan did in tempting Eve was to convince her the Word of God should not take root in her heart.

What argument did Satan use with Eve? (Genesis 3:5)

_____

_____

_____

What did Jesus say to combat Satan? (Matthew 4:4, 7, 10)

_____

What are we given to keep Satan from harming us? (Ephesians 6:11)

_____

4. The Stony Heart

Rocky soil is not hard to find in Israel. Men have worked for generations picking rocks out of the fields, using them to build fences and houses, so the fields can be plowed to receive seed.

Seed that falls on rocky soil may be wedged in a crack under a rock and quickly sprout. But since the soil is shallow, and the seed is unable to put down roots, it quickly dies in the hot sun.

What does the rocky soil represent in this parable? (Matthew 13:20-21)

_____

_____

_____

What two things often cause the "shallow Christian" to wither up and die after first receiving the Gospel? (Matthew 13:21)

1. _____

2. _____

The Bible calls those who accept God's truth, then turn away from it, "backsliders."

Why do some people "backslide" after having first received God's truth into their lives? (Matthew 13:21)

_____

What warning did God give Israel about this? (Deuteronomy 8:11-14)

_____

_____

_____

What happens to the person who does what he wants to apart from God's way? (Proverbs 14:12)

_____

If a man is determined to turn away from God, will God exalt him if he calls out to the Most High? (Hosea 11:7)

_____ Yes

_____ No

What happens if we deny (disown) God? (II Timothy 2:12)

_____

Jesus told a story of a person who swept a house clean of demons, but did not fill the house with the Holy Spirit after it had been cleansed.

What can we do to keep each other from backsliding? (Hebrews 3:12-13)

_____

Is it possible for a person who once received the Gospel, then deliberately turned his back on God, to be restored to salvation? (Hebrews 6:4-6)

_____

5. **The Cluttered Life**

Besides rocks, Israel is renowned for briers and thorns. Poor soil often produces thorns. In this parable some of the seed fell among thorns, perhaps at the edge of the field where the ground had not been plowed and fertilized.

What happened to the seed that fell in the thorn bushes? (Matthew 13:7)

_____

What two things did Jesus mention that choke the life out of the Gospel? (Matthew 13:22)

1. _____

2. _____

Jesus knew that anxiety and worry are two of the huge briers which choke the life out of God's people. Therefore he spent a lot of time talking about the foolishness of worry.

What can you accomplish by worry and anxiety? (Matthew 6:25-30) (check correct answers)

_____ You can make yourself taller.

_____ You can get a new wardrobe.

_____ You can put food on your table.

_____ You can get out of prison.

_____ You can undo the mistakes of the past.

_____ You can get someone to love you.

_____ You can put off tomorrow.

_____ None of the above.

One of the results of worry is insomnia. God says it is useless to get up early or stay up late in order to worry.

What does God give His children? (Psalm 127:2)

_____

Jesus' second example of the thorns which choke out the truth of God is "the deceitfulness of wealth."

Does Jesus say it is wrong to make money? (Matthew 13:22)

_____ Yes

_____ No

Riches are not wrong. But riches deceive. They cause us to think we can do anything in our own power because we have money. Therefore, it is far better to be poor and righteous than to be rich and deceived.

What happens to the person who trusts in riches? (Proverbs 11:28)

_____

Do riches make it easier or harder to enter the kingdom of heaven? (Matthew 19:23)

_____ Easier

_____ Harder

What did Jesus say about rich people getting into heaven? (Matthew 19:24)

_____

_____

_____

If the possession of riches makes it difficult to enter the kingdom of heaven, why then do people want to be rich—unless they are wrapped up with the briers of the "deceitfulness of riches"?

What should we be seeking rather than riches? (Matthew 6:33)

_____

What is called "great gain" in the Bible? (I Timothy 6:6)

_____

Is money the root of all evil? (I Timothy 6:10)

_____ Yes, money is the root of all evil.

_____ No, it's the love of money, not money itself.

Paul tells the man of God to flee love of money and set his heart on something else.

What should the man of God desire rather than money? (I Timothy 6:11)

1. _____
2. _____
3. _____
4. _____
5. _____
6. _____

Where did Jesus say we should be storing our treasures? (Matthew 6:20)

_____

Jesus said money was often a master, causing us to do all sorts of things to serve it.

What did Jesus say would happen if we tried to serve the masters of God and money at the same time? (Matthew 6:24)

_____

_____

_____

What becomes of those who scorn instruction? (Proverbs 13:13)

_____

Jesus told the pharisees that they canceled out the Word of God—actually making it null and void.

What was the big briar in the lives of the Pharisees which choked out the Word of God? (Mark 7:9, 13)

_____ Adultery

_____ Hate

_____ Stealing from widows and orphans

_____ Murder

_____ Rebellion

_____ Tradition

Paul told Timothy that a time would come when men would no longer love the Word of God and would only want teachers who would say the things they wanted to hear—rather than what God wanted them to hear.

What would they want these teachers to do? (II Timothy 4:3)

_____ Fill their bellies with the food the swine were eating.

_____ Say what their itching ears want to hear.

_____ Lead them astray with silly women.

_____ Let them lie down on beds of ivory.

6. Spiritual Fruit

The final seed the sower threw into the field fell into good soil—soil that had been plowed, fertilized, and softened by the rain.

What kind of crop did this seed produce? (Matthew 13:8)

_____

_____

Who is represented by the seed that fell into good soil? (Matthew 13:23)

_____

How often should we think about the Word of God? (Psalms 1:2)

_____

If we let the Word of God take root in our heart, what can we expect in return? (Joshua 1:8)

_____

_____

What happens when the words of Jesus abide (remain) in us? (John 15:7)

_____

_____

_____

Why is the Word of God given to us? (John 20:31)

_____

_____

_____

What happens when we hear the Word of God and keep it? (Luke 11:28)

_____

Jesus said those who kept His word would be real disciples.

What did He say the truth of His word would do to people? (John 8:31-32)

_____

WRAP UP

God's Word will not return unto Him void. It will take root, somewhere, in someone. If our lives are hard, we need to submit them to the plow. If the soil of our lives is rocky, we need to be willing to let someone help us get rid of the rocks. If our lives are cluttered with briers that choke out the Gospel, we may need to have our field burned off before planting time. God wants to plant His seed in our hearts.

FINAL LESSON

This parable was not given to be heard—it was given to be acted on. Jesus closes out the parable by saying, "He who has ears to hear, let him hear." There is a difference between hearers and doers. Jesus wants His followers to act on both the warnings and the promises of this parable.

PERSONAL REVIEW QUESTIONS

Circle T (true) or F (false)

1. T F God scatters His Word on all kinds of soil.

2. T F The birds in this parable represent Satan.

3. T F The hard soil represents hearts and minds which are hardened to God's truth.

4.   T   F   The reason the seed that fell on rocky soil died was it could not find room to take root.

5.   T   F   Jesus said the briers of worry and the deceitfulness of riches often choke out the Gospel.

6.   T   F   Jesus said it was okay to be rich as long as you had a little camel.

7.   T   F   Jesus never did condemn riches, but he did say money often got in the way of God.

8.   T   F   If you let the Gospel take root in your life it will bear good fruit.

9.   T   F   This parable is about different soils as much as about the sower and his seed.

10.   T   F   God wants to sow His seed in our hearts.

MEMORY VERSE

Matthew 6:24 (Memorize, then write it on these lines.)

_____

_____

_____

_____

TRUE OR FALSE ANSWERS:

1-T, 2-T, 3-T, 4-T, 5-T, 6-F, 7-T, 8-T, 9-T, 10-T

NOTES

Lesson 7

The Parable of the Good Samaritan

"Who is My Neighbor?"

SCRIPTURE: Luke 10:25-37
VIDEO REFERENCE: Lesson #7
SUPPLEMENTARY READING REFERENCE:
> *Ten Parables of Jesus: Poking Holes in Religious Balloons*
> Chapter VII: "The Parable of the Good Samaritan"

1. Introduction

It began with a question, the kind of question asked by those who don't want an answer. It was asked by someone who thought he knew the answer. The one asking the question was a religious Jew, an expert in the law of Moses. Such men were sometimes called lawyers, sometimes called scribes. They were people who had mastered the Jewish law found in the first five books of the Bible, or Torah.

List the first five books of the Bible

1. _____
2. _____
3. _____
4. _____
5. _____

What was the question the religious Jew asked Jesus? (Luke 10:25)

_____

_____

Jesus responded, as He often did, by answering the question with another question—forcing the religious Jew, who was trying to trap Him, to answer instead.

What was the question Jesus asked? (Luke 10:26)

_____

_____

The religious Jew answered by quoting two Old Testament scriptures.

What was the first scripture he quoted? (Deuteronomy 6:5)

_____

_____

_____

_____

What was the second scripture he quoted? (Leviticus 19:18)

_____

_____

_____

_____

Jesus commended the man, but added a touch of sarcasm. He knew the man was not interested in the truth; he was only trying to trap Jesus by forcing Him to give an answer that went against the Old Testament law. Thus, after the expert had answered correctly, using scriptures from the Torah, Jesus nailed him.

"It's not enough to answer correctly if you want eternal life," He said in essence. "You must do the law—not just quote it—in order to live."

Backed into a corner, the religious Jew knew Jesus had put him on the spot. But he was not finished yet. The law said "Love your neighbor." This man, though, loved no one because the law did not tell him specifically who to love. So he lashed back with a loaded question—a question designed so the lawyer could say "Gottcha!" when Jesus answered wrongly.

What was the final question the Jew asked Jesus? (Luke 10:29)

_____

_____

One can almost hear Jesus chuckling with, "I thought you would never ask." In answer to the man's question, He tells what is the most perfect short story every told—the Parable of the Good Samaritan.

The story deals with the question asked by the religious Jew: "Who is my neighbor?" It is a story of social relationships.

As a point of interest it should be noted that in the very beginning of history, God never asked questions. He spoke directly and man spoke back directly. There was no need for questions, for there was no sin in the world. Everything was perfectly clear.

Who asked the first question in the history of mankind? (Genesis 3:1)

_____

_____

Ever since Satan brought darkness into the world by tempting Eve to question God's authority, mankind has been walking in confusion—asking questions. For centuries, the Jews had been debating the question concerning who to love and who not to love. The result: most of them loved no one. The question this religious Jew asked was similar in nature to the rhetorical question Cain, Adam's son, arrogantly asked God.

What had Cain just done? (Genesis 4:8)

_____

When God asked Cain where his brother, Abel, was, Cain replied with an insolent question of his own.

What was Cain's question/reply to God? (Genesis 4:9)

_____

_____

Cain was defending himself for murdering his brother. The religious Jew was defending himself for not loving his neighbor.

Jesus had confirmed the Jew's answer that to have eternal life you should love God and love your neighbor. Now Jesus is getting ready to point out you cannot love God unless you love your neighbor.

What is the message God has given us from the beginning? (I John 3:11)

_____

How do we know we have eternal life? (I John 3:14)

_____

How much should we love our brothers? (I John 3:16)

_____

_____

What was the popular Jewish teaching concerning loving your neighbor? (Matthew 5:43)

_____

_____

Is it possible to love God and not love each other? (I John 4:7,8)

_____ Yes

_____ No

2. The Setting of the Parable

The city of Jerusalem sits at an altitude of 2,300 feet above sea level. The city of Jericho, less than 20 miles away, is 1,300 feet below sea level. The road from Jerusalem to Jericho, called "The Jericho Road," drops 3,600 feet and runs through the Judean wilderness, one of the most desolate areas on earth. Jesus used this road as the setting for His parable.

3. The Characters of the Parable

Like all good short stories, this parable has a marvelous cast of characters. Before you go any further, read Luke 10:30-35, then list the cast of characters.

1. _____
2. _____
3. _____
4. _____
5. _____
6. _____

4. The Traveler

Only a fool, an egotist, or a desperate man would venture down the notorious Jericho Road alone. Wise men knew always to travel in caravans. If the elements or some wild animal didn't kill you, you were in mortal danger from the thieves and robbers who hid in the many caves waiting for some fool, egotist, or desperate man to come along so they could separate him from his money and belongings. Undoubtedly, this man knew better than to venture out alone. He had probably been warned. Therefore, to some extent, anything that happened to him out there was his own fault.

5. The Robbers

A lot of people operate on a principle that the only reason you have anything is so they can take it away from you. If someone flashes money in a crowd, there is always someone whose first reaction is, "How can I get that away from him?" Instead of working for a living, they spend their time stealing that which others work for. They are the pickpockets, robbers, thieves, extortionists, blackmailers, bandits, brigands, and hustlers of the world. They still wait along all the Jericho Roads of life, ready to take advantage of the fools, egotists, desperate and innocent people of the world.

What did the robbers take from the man besides his money, his donkey, and his pack? (Luke 10:30)

_____

What did they do to him besides taking his stuff? (Luke 10:30)

_____

6. The Priest

The first man to pass along the road was a priest.

The traveller looked dead. The only way to know whether he was alive or dead was to take his pulse, feel for his heartbeat—to touch him. However, the law that the priest lived by was very specific about what would happen if a priest touched a dead man.

What would the priest have to do if he touched the man and found him dead? (Numbers 19:11-13)

_____

_____

_____

_____

What did the priest do when he saw the man lying in the ditch beside the road? (Luke 10:31)

_____

7. The Levite

The Levite was in the same situation as the priest. His motto was "safety first."

Rather than run the risk of being attacked himself, what did he do? (Luke 10:32)

_____

8. The Samaritan

Now Jesus adds one of those wonderful twists to His story. He injects a totally foreign character. A despised character. While the Samaritans lived in the same nation as the Jews—in an area known as Samaria—they were of a mixed race and had what was to the Jews a totally unacceptable approach to God. By inserting a Samaritan as the hero of His story, Jesus strikes a mortal blow at racism and religious discrimination.

What was the heart reaction of the Samaritan when he saw the half-dead man? (Luke 10:33)

_____

List five ways in which the Samaritan showed his love. (Luke 10:34)

1. _____
2. _____
3. _____
4. _____
5. _____

What extra thing did the Samaritan do in the man's behalf? (Luke 10:35)

_____

_____

Jesus finished His story by asking a final question.

What was the final question? (Luke 10:36)

_____

_____

_____

To whom was the question addressed? (Luke 10:37)

_____

The lawyer was unable to bring himself to use the hated word "Samaritan."

How did the lawyer respond? (Luke 10:37)

_____

_____

At this point Jesus repeated something He had said earlier.

What had He said earlier? (Luke 10:28)

_____

What did He say again? (Luke 10:37)

_____

WRAP UP

In this cast of characters we find the three basic approaches to life. (Fill in the blanks.)

The robbers said, "What's thine is _____, I'll take it."

The priest and the Levite said, "What's mine is _____, I'll keep it."

The Samaritan said, "What's mine is _____, I'll give it."

Which one of these approaches to life describes you?

FINAL LESSON

Four things need to be noticed from this parable:

(1) Very few people, even top religious leaders, love their neighbor enough to inconvenience themselves for him—much less die for him.

(2) "Neighbor," in God's vocabulary, is more than the person who lives next to us, or even someone we know—he is anyone who crosses our path.

(3) Love is shown by meeting people's needs.

(4) Often the ones who show Christian love are the ones the world has cast out. Since God does not judge on nationality, race, religion, sex, or handicap, neither should we.

PERSONAL REVIEW QUESTIONS

Circle T (true) or F (false)

1. T   F   Jewish "lawyers" were members of the bar.

2. T   F   If we love God and love our neighbor, even if we don't act it out, we'll have eternal life.

3. T   F   Jesus was really hard on the traveler because the guy knew better than to get himself in this mess.

4. T   F   Jesus said, "Robbers you have with you always."

5. T   F   Sometimes a person is justified in leaving a man in the ditch if the fellow brings it on himself.

6. T   F   If you have important duties in the temple it's okay to leave a man in a ditch.

7. T   F   If you're in a hurry it's okay to leave a man in the ditch, since the next person will probably stop to help.

8. T   F   The Samaritan stopped to help because he knew the Jews would reward him.

9. T   F   It's not enough to know how to love; God expects us to act it out.

10. T   F   The Bible has nothing to say about racial prejudice.

11. T   F   Godly people are not always religious.

12. T   F   God wants us to be friends to anyone in need as long as it does not cause us inconvenience.

MEMORY VERSE

I John 3:16 (Memorize, then write it on these lines.)

_____

_____

_____

_____

TRUE OR FALSE ANSWERS:

1-F, 2-F, 3-F, 4-F, 5-F, 6-F, 7-F, 8-F, 9-T, 10-F, 11-T, 12-F

NOTES

Lesson 8

The Parable of the Rich Fool

"Eat, Drink and Be Merry...but Tomorrow You Die."

SCRIPTURE: Luke 12:13-21
VIDEO REFERENCE: Lesson #8
SUPPLEMENTARY READING REFERENCE:
  Ten Parables of Jesus: Poking Holes in Religious Balloons
  Chapter VIII: "The Parable of the Rich Fool"

1. The Problem of the Man

Jesus had just finished instructing His disciples, in the hearing of a crowd numbering in the thousands, to keep their minds and hearts centered on spiritual priorities. To concentrate on anything else—especially money (or the lack of it)—brings anxiety.

Most of our anxieties are related to money. We are more concerned about money than our health. In fact, most people see money as the key to health, for if we are rich we can hire a doctor, rent a nursing home, pay for medical supplies. If we have money we can get the best lawyer, which sometimes is the difference between prison or freedom, life or death. Transportation, communication, career—all hinge on money.

Jesus was teaching about these things, urging people to focus on God—who is the provider of all things.

Who does Jesus say will give you the right words to say in times of crisis? (Luke 12:12)

_____ A friend

_____ An angel

_____ A lawyer

_____ The Holy Spirit

Jesus said it is unnecessary to worry about our well being. If God is controlling our lives, we are going to be taken care of.

Whom should we not fear? (Luke 12:4)

_____

_____

Whom should we fear? (Luke 12:5)

_____

_____

Jesus said man is of great worth and value to God; therefore, we should not fear or be afraid.

What does God care for that is worth far less than man? (Luke 12:6-7)

_____

As He was teaching, a fellow in the crowd—who obviously had not heard a thing Jesus had said—blurted out.

What did the man want Jesus to do? (Luke 12:13)

_____

_____

Jesus refused to be a judge or referee, deciding who would get what among quarreling brothers. He had more important things to do than arbitrate over inherited money. In fact, that was just what He had been talking about—warning the people about focusing on money and all the problems it brings.

What did Jesus warn the people to be on guard against? (Luke 12:15)

_____

What is it life does not consist of? (Luke 12:15)

_____

_____

In Luke 16 Jesus tells another parable of a wealthy farmer whose foreman was lazy, not collecting the farmer's debts as he should. The farmer threatened to fire the foreman, who then went to the people who owed him money and negotiated payment.

How did the farmer feel about his foreman's actions? (Luke 16:8)

_____

A steward is one who takes care of other people's things. In the kingdom of God, good stewardship means taking care of the things—and the money—God has given you. God wants His people to prosper financially, but only if they are willing to be good stewards of that prosperity. Thus, God may withhold riches from us until He is certain we will be good stewards. But riches are not sinful—they are blessings from God.

Nowhere does the Bible teach that riches are evil. Just the opposite. The Bible teaches that riches, or wealth, are essentially good.

List the seven good things that belong by eternal right to the Lord Jesus. (Revelation 5:12)

1. _____
2. _____
3. _____
4. _____
5. _____
6. _____
7. _____

Where do riches and honor come from? (I Chronicles 29:12)

_____

God is the ultimate source of riches and honor. Anything that originates from God must be good in itself. But none of these things come if we seek them for themselves.

What are we to seek rather than money? (Matthew 6:33)

_____

Some people, including prisoners, own nothing.

Are such people free from the obligations of stewardship?

_____ Yes

_____ No

List things we are responsible for besides money—things we should be good stewards of.

_____

_____

_____

_____

_____

_____

2. The Parable of Jesus

As with many of Jesus' parables, this one grew out of a familiar farming situation. The Old Testament promises of God's blessing included long life, healthy children, and good crops. The Jews were an agrarian society. Many of them were farmers and shepherds. Long years, good crops, and many sons to plow the crops meant you were blessed by God.

How had God blessed the man in Jesus' parable? (Luke 12:16)

_____

_____

In telling the story Jesus makes it plain the crops were not accidental. The crops were evidence of God's blessing. They were God's gift to the man.

What was the natural question the man asked? (Luke 12:17)

_____

_____

List several things the man could have done with his crops rather than store them in barns.

1. _____

_____

2. _____

_____

3. _____

_____

4. _____

_____

According to the Law of Moses, what part of his crops belonged to God in a special way? (Leviticus 27:30)

_____

Which portion of his crops should he tithe? (Numbers 18:29)

_____

What did God require him to do with the tithe of his crops? (Malachi 3:10)

_____

_____

What did God promise would happen to him if he tithed his crops? (Malachi 3:10-12)

1. _____

   _____

2. _____

   _____

3. _____

   _____

4. _____

   _____

5. _____

   _____

Did the man consider doing any of the above? (Luke 12:18)

_____ Yes

_____ No

The farmer seemed to be living as though God did not exist. Perhaps he felt the land was obligated to produce good crops. Perhaps he felt it was luck or chance that his land produced good crops. Maybe he felt the land produced good crops because he worked hard and made it happen.

Who did the man say the crops belonged to? (Luke 12:17)

_____

What did the man decide he should do with God's blessing? (Luke 12:18)

_____

_____

We find a similar situation of poor stewardship in another parable Jesus told. In that parable a man had also received a blessing from his king, just as this farmer had received a blessing from God.

What did the man do with his blessing? (Matthew 25:18)

_____

_____

What did God want him to do with his blessing? (Matthew 25:16, 27)

_____

_____

What happened to him because he hoarded his blessing? (Matthew 25:28-30)

   1. _____

      _____

   2. _____

      _____

In reality, the abundant crops were a gift from God.

What should we do with our God-given gifts? (I Peter 4:10)

_____

_____

God is not saying it is wrong to store up for the future. The problem comes when we fail to recognize God as the source.

Where do good gifts come from? (James 1:17)

_____

Describe the man's attitude toward his possessions. (Luke 12:17-19) (Check correct answers)

_____ Greed

_____ Generosity

_____ Gratefulness

_____ Gratitude

_____ Anxiety

While God does not condemn saving, as long as it is part of a long range program of stewardship, He says the greatest blessings are reserved for those who live to give, rather than live to get—for that is the nature of God.

Those who live to get are constantly worried they will not get enough.

What did Jesus tell the young ruler to do with his riches? (Matthew 19:21)

_____

_____

Why was the young ruler unable to follow Jesus? (Matthew 19:22)

_____

What did God call the rich farmer who thought he could live on riches alone? (Luke 12:20)

_____

What does God say will happen to our riches if we hoard them and do not use them to help others? (James 4:3)

_____

_____

_____

WRAP UP

The rich farmer made three mistakes:

(1) He mistook man for God. He ruled God out of his life.

What does the Bible call the man who lives as if there is no God? (Psalm 14:1)

_____

(2) He mistook his body for his soul. He did not understand that real riches cannot be stored in barns.

Where did Jesus say real riches are stored? (Matthew 6:19-20)

_____

(3) He mistook time for eternity. He thought he could control the future.

What does the Bible say about the length of our lives? (James 4:14)

_____

_____

Instead of saying to himself, "You have plenty of good things laid up for many years," what should he have said? (James 4:15)

_____

_____

FINAL LESSON

What really counts is not how much we leave behind, but how much we've sent on before.

PERSONAL REVIEW QUESTIONS

Circle T (true) or F (false)

1. T F Jesus hated to talk about money.

2. T F Jesus had a lot to say about money.

3. T F Jesus indicated that money is at the root of most of our anxieties.

4. T F Money can buy our way to happiness.

5. T F Money can make it easier to get to heaven.

6. T F Rich men have a tough time getting into heaven.

7. T F Money is a gift from God.

8. T F Those who have a lot of money also have a lot of responsibility to use it for God.

9. T F Money is given to us so we can use it to help others.

10. T F All saving is wrong.

11.   T   F   Hoarding for self alone is wrong.

12.   T   F   Money can buy us length of life.

13.   T   F   God doesn't care what we do with our time as long as we tithe our income.

14.   T   F   Biblical stewardship deals only with money.

15.   T   F   We are just as responsible to be good stewards of our bodies as we are to be good stewards of our money.

MEMORY VERSE

James 4:14 (Memorize, then write it on these lines.)

_____

_____

_____

_____

TRUE OR FALSE ANSWERS:

1-F, 2-T, 3-T, 4-F, 5-F, 6-T, 7-T, 8-T, 9-T, 10-F, 11-T, 12-F, 13-F, 14-F, 15-T.

NOTES

Lesson 9

The Parable of Two Men in the Temple

God Listens to the Broken Heart

SCRIPTURE: Luke 18:9-14
VIDEO REFERENCE: Lesson #9
SUPPLEMENTARY READING REFERENCE:

Ten Parables of Jesus: Poking Holes in Religious Balloons
Chapter IX: "The Parable of Two Men in the Temple"

1. Two Extremes

The Pharisees: More than 150 years before the birth of Christ, the nation of Israel was under the control of Syria. After much suffering, a small band of Jews, following Judas the Maccabee, revolted. This turned into a full-scale revolution which drove the Syrians out of Israel. As often follows a revolution, corruption set in. When that happened, a group of religious Jews, called Pharisees, separated themselves from the government and vowed to live holy, separate lives.

The Pharisees avoided contact with anything which would make them ritually impure. They kept all the laws of Moses as well as the interpretations of those laws called the Oral Law, or Talmud. By the time of Jesus, they had become a law unto themselves, feeling that because they were so pious they, alone, had access to God.

The Publicans: Shortly after the Syrians were driven from the land, the Romans occupied Israel. They selected certain Jews who were willing to cooperate with the Romans to collect taxes for them. These tax collectors, or "publicans," were looked upon with hate and scorn by the Jews who felt they had betrayed their own people for money. Not only were the publicans collaborating with the hated occupation forces, they had the authority to persecute their own people—often collecting twice the amount of taxes due so they could line their own pockets.

Jesus loved to line up extremes in His parables. In one parable, He contrasted a priest and Levite against a hated Samaritan. In another, He contrasted a prodigal son against a self-righteous son. In this parable, He contrasted a pharisee against a tax-collector.

To whom was this story told? (Luke 18:9)

_____

_____

The Bible has much to say about self-righteousness. In fact, it seems there are two things which stand between man and God: carnal sin and self-righteous religion.

What did God say deceives self-righteous people? (Obadiah 3)

_____

What becomes of those who exalt themselves? (Luke 14:11)

_____

_____

What did the Pharisees think about Jesus? (John 9:13-16, 24)

_____

_____

_____

What did Jesus say about the Pharisees? (Luke 16:15)

_____

_____

Who did Jesus say the Pharisees were descendants of? (Matthew 23:31)

_____

_____

What were the two men, the Pharisee and the Publican, doing in the temple? (Luke 18:10)

_____

2. **The Prayer of the Pharisee**

   What should we be seeking in prayer? (Psalm 27:8)

   _____

   _____

Who are we to call on in prayer? (Isaiah 55:6)

_____

_____

What was the Pharisee doing in his prayer? (Luke 18:11)

_____

Is it proper to ask God for various things? (Philippians 4:6)

_____ No, to ask God for anything is begging.

_____ Yes, God wants us to ask Him for everything.

Prayer is communion with God. We do not need to remind God how good we are; we need to ask Him for help.

What were the three things Jesus told His disciples they should ask of God? (Matthew 6:11-13)

1. _____

_____

2. _____

_____

3. _____

_____

What did the Pharisee ask of God? (Luke 18:11-12)

_____ He asked for guidance in his life.

_____ He asked for healing.

_____ He asked for daily bread.

_____ He asked God to help him with his weaknesses.

_____ He asked God to forgive him for sinning.

_____ He asked for nothing because he felt he was perfect.

How long should our prayers be? (Ecclesiastes 5:2)

_____

Who should we allow to pray through us? (Romans 8:26)

_____

What did Jesus call the Pharisees? (Matthew 23:23)

_____ Idiots

_____ Criminals

_____ Hypocrites

Did Jesus condemn them for righteous living? (Matthew 23:23)

_____ Yes, He said they were wrong to keep the law.

_____ No, He said they should keep the law but change their attitude.

What did Jesus say were the important matters of the law? (Matthew 23:23)

1. _____
2. _____
3. _____

Jesus warned against religion that makes us look good on the outside but leaves the inside full of sin.

How did Jesus describe the religion of the Pharisees? (Matthew 23:27)

_____

_____

_____

_____

What did Jesus say was inside the Pharisees? (Matthew 23:28)

1. _____
2. _____

The Pharisee bragged that he fasted twice a week. Jesus said men should fast, but not the way the Pharisee did.

How should we fast? (Matthew 6:17-18)

_____

_____

_____

_____

The Pharisee bragged that he tithed his income. Jesus said men should tithe, but not the way the Pharisee did.

How should we give? (Matthew 6:2-4)

_____

_____

_____

_____

The Pharisee prayed out loud in the Temple so others could hear him. Jesus said men should pray, but not the way the Pharisee did.

How should we pray? (Matthew 6:5-6)

_____

_____

_____

_____

Read through the "Lord's Prayer" in Matthew 6:9-13.

Did the Pharisee pray for any of the things Jesus taught His disciples to pray for?

_____ Yes

_____ No

3. **The Prayer of the Publican**

What position did the tax collector take when he prayed? (Luke 18:13)

1. _____

2. _____

3. _____

What did the tax collector ask for? (Luke 18:13)

_____

_____

How would you describe the tax collector's prayer? (Luke 18:13)
(Check correct answers)

_____ Long

_____ Short

_____ From his mind

_____ From his heart

_____ Prayed so others could hear

_____ Prayed so God could hear

_____ Bragging

_____ Confessing

Does God know our needs before we ask Him? (Matthew 6:8)

_____ No, God only knows if we tell Him.

_____ Yes, God knows everything.

WRAP UP

The Pharisee used the occasion of prayer to (1) brag before others, (2) condemn others, (3) compare himself with others, and (4) justify himself.

The publican used the occasion of prayer to ask God for help.

FINAL LESSON

Jesus said the prayer of the tax collector was a prayer of true repentance, for it is the prayer of a heart-broken man. That is the kind of prayer God loves to hear and answer.

PERSONAL REVIEW QUESTIONS

Circle T (true) or F (false)

1. T   F   Jesus condemned people who prayed out loud.

2. T   F   Jesus condemned people who fasted.

3. T   F   Jesus condemned people who tithed their income.

4. T   F   Jesus said God looks at our hearts, not our outward appearance.

5. T   F   Jesus said God answers true prayers of repentance.

6. T   F   Jesus said lengthy prayers are useless if our hearts are full of pride.

7. T   F   True prayer seeks the face of God.

8. T   F   Jesus said it was wrong to pray in the temple.

9. T   F   It is wrong to pray for personal needs.

10. T   F   The best prayers are the ones the Holy Spirit prays through us.

MEMORY VERSE

Matthew 6:9-13 (Memorize, then write them on these lines.)

_____

_____

_____

_____

_____

_____

_____

TRUE OR FALSE ANSWERS:

1-F, 2-F, 3-F, 4-T, 5-T, 6-T, 7-T, 8-F, 9-F, 10-T

NOTES

Lesson 10

The Parable of the Prodigal Son

Welcome Home!

SCRIPTURE: Luke 15:11-32
VIDEO REFERENCE: Lesson #10
SUPPLEMENTARY READING REFERENCE:
   Ten Parables of Jesus: Poking Holes in Religious Balloons
   Chapter X: "The Parable of the Prodigal Son"

1. Introduction

Any teacher who tells a story takes a risk with the person who hears that story. Jesus was such a storyteller. He knew that His stories would be received with mixed reaction. Some people would simply not understand and would go away scratching their heads. Others would misunderstand and twist the meaning to justify what they were doing, rather than changing—as Jesus intended for them to do. Still others would understand exactly what He was saying and react with anger, for they would realize He was threatening their lifestyle, doctrine, or traditions. A few, however, would understand and be inspired to change their way of life and therefore become more like God. Jesus wanted everyone to respond that way, but He was wise enough to know the majority would respond in one of the other ways.

One day Jesus was sitting with a group of tax collectors and "sinners." Tax collectors were Jewish citizens who took advantage of the Roman occupation of Palestine for their own financial gain. For a fee, they had purchased a franchise which authorized them to collect taxes from their own people. In fact, they not only collected taxes, but used threat and extortion to collect huge sums over and above the taxes due—which they kept for themselves. In return they received personal protection from Rome.

That afternoon the group gathered around Jesus was relaxed, eating and drinking together. These "undesirables" were listening intently to what Jesus was saying about the kingdom of God. Remember, He did not teach like the scribes and pharisees, who quoted the ancient rabbis as their authority. Those who heard Jesus knew He was an authority within Himself.

But the pharisees and teachers of the law were offended, angry—not so much with what Jesus was saying, for they weren't really listening. They were angered that He, a recognized Jewish teacher, was eating and drinking with people they considered to be riff-raff.

It was in response to their anger that Jesus told three short stories. All had to do with things that were lost, and the joy that should accompany the finding.

What were the three things which were lost? (Luke 15:4, 8, 11-13)

1. _____

2. _____

3. _____

The stories are told with no follow-up dialogue or any record of questions from the hearers. Nor does Luke say anything about any response from the hearers—although we should assume it was heard by the tax collectors as well as the pharisees.

Before you go any further, picture yourself as one of the tax collectors sitting around Jesus that afternoon. Try to imagine the kind of life they led and the way they felt. Now read the entire 15th chapter of Luke. Remember, there is no recorded response.

How do you think the "sinners" would have responded to Jesus' stories?

_____

_____

_____

_____

How do you think the Pharisees would have responded?

_____

_____

_____

_____

When you look at the three parables together you find several common threads running through them.

What is identical about the single sheep, the coin, and the younger son? (Luke 15:4, 8, 24)

_____

What was the identical reaction of the shepherd, the woman, and the father? (Luke 15:6, 9, 23)

_____

2. The Parable

The parable of the prodigal son is the most unforgettable of all Jesus' stories. It is both forceful and tender. It is true to life. It is filled with exciting characters, all of whom are like people we know. Pretend you are the casting director of a stage production and you are in charge of lining up the characters to play the roles in this story.

Who are the major characters in the story? (Luke 15:12, 22, 28)

1. _____

2. _____

3. _____

List some of the minor characters. (Luke 15:13, 15, 22)

1. _____

2. _____

3. _____

4. _____

How many sons did the father have? (Luke 15:11)

_____

As Jesus was looking at His audience, who did the younger son represent?

_____

Who did the elder son represent?

_____

Who did the father represent?

_____

3. The Younger Son

Under Jewish law, a father was supposed to divide his inheritance after he died, with two thirds going to the elder son and one third to the younger. But this younger son had problems. He didn't want to wait until his dad died. He wanted his share of the inheritance as soon as he came of age.

While the father could divide up the "living" and give it to his son, he could not impart to him "life." Life comes only when one is re-born, or in the words of this parable, when he "comes to himself." The younger son could not get that from his father. He had to find it on his own.

What's the best word to describe the younger son's attitude?

_____ Wise

_____ Selfless

_____ Rebellious

_____ Submissive

_____ Mean

What does the Bible have to say about rebellion? (I Samuel 15:23)

_____

_____

God seldom says "no" or blocks our way when we start out to do foolish things. Like any wise father, He allows us to find our own way. The possession of material things, while important to mortals, is never a priority to God. In this case the father did nothing to interfere with the boy's headstrong determination to do things his own way.

What did the younger son do with the money his father gave him? (Luke 15:13)

_____ Invested part of it in interest-bearing bonds and lived off the rest.

_____ Bought real estate.

_____ Used it for college tuition.

_____ Blew it.

What circumstances occurred to force the younger son to take action? (Luke 15:14)

_____ His conscience began to bother him.

_____ He had a great job offer.

_____ His father called him and begged him to change his life.

_____ He met a girl and she inspired him to a higher way of living.

_____ He had a dream about his poor old mother.

_____ He ran out of money and food.

After he lost his money, the younger son was forced to do something he had refused to do at home.

What was the younger son forced to do? (Luke 15:15)

_____

_____

The Bible has a good bit to say about labor.

What did God tell Adam about the relationship between working and eating? (Genesis 3:19)

_____

_____

What did Paul tell the lazy Christians in Thessalonica about work? (II Thessalonians 3:10)

_____

_____

What kind of example did Paul set before the Thessalonians concerning work? (II Thessalonians 3:7-9)

_____

_____

_____

When writing to the church at Ephesus, a church which had many people who had formerly made their living by stealing, Paul had some strong words about the new way of life Jesus had for them.

What did Paul tell the Ephesians about the reason for honest labor? (Ephesians 4:28)

_____

_____

_____

After the younger son had gotten a job with a pig farmer, he continued to be hungry because of the famine in the land.

What did he have to eat? (Luke 15:16)

_____

_____

What do you think had become of all his friends who so willingly spent his money when he was throwing his father's inheritance around in "riotous living"? (Luke 15:16)

_____

Backbreaking work often causes a person to think straight for the first time in his life.

What happened to the prodigal son as he was eating with the pigs in the pig pen? (Luke 15:17)

_____

_____

The prodigal made some resolutions in the pig pen.

List these resolutions. (Luke 15:18-19)

1. _____

2. _____

3. _____

4. _____

When the progidal son left home he did so with a rebellious arrogance, as if to say, "Leave me alone. I can do anything I want." But now he had reached a painful conclusion. He said, "I am no longer worthy to be called your son. . . " (Luke 15:19).

Why do you think the prodigal son changed his mind?

_____

_____

_____

_____

After he planned what he would say, what did the prodigal son do? (Luke 15:20)

_____

_____

Under what conditions was the boy willing to come home?

_____ If he could be reinstated as son and heir.

_____ If he could be put in charge of the servants.

_____ Willing to do whatever the father asked him to do.

4. The Father

Remember, this is but one story in a trilogy of short stories. While all three stories deal with things lost and found—i.e., sheep, coin, son—they are really not about the lost items, but about the ones who find the items. Therefore, the first story is not about a lost sheep; it is about a good shepherd. The second story is not about a lost coin; it is about an industrious woman who does not give up. This third story, while known traditionally as the parable of the prodigal son, is actually the parable of the loving father.

When the prodigal son started home, his father, perhaps standing in the watchtower in the vineyard or olive grove, saw him first.

What did the father do? (Luke 15:20)

_____

_____

_____

Why is God (the father) described as running? (Luke 15:20)

_____

_____

Immediately the son started off into his rehearsed speech. However, he never got to the part about "Make me as one of your hired servants." The father cut him off halfway though the speech.

What did the son say that let the father know there had been a change in his life? (Luke 15:21)

_____

_____

When the son left home he did so in rebellion to the father, saying he could no longer live under his father's rules.

What does he now want to do? (Luke 15:19)

_____

_____

How would you describe the prodigal's changed attitude?
(Check correct answers.)

_____ Submissive

_____ Repentant

_____ Humble

What did the father require the prodigal to do before he could receive him back home? (Luke 15:20-22)
(Check correct answers).

_____ Take a bath.

_____ Cut his hair.

_____ Sober up.

_____ Spend three years on probation.

_____ Pay his debt to society first.

_____ Change his clothes.

_____ Pay back the money he'd wasted.

_____ Tell his elder brother he was sorry.

_____ Admit he'd goofed up and ask to come home.

The father told his servants to do five things.

What did the father tell the servants to do? (Luke 15:22-23)

1. _____

2. _____

3. _____

4. _____

5. _____

What do each of these things mean to you?

1. The best robe: _____

_____

_____

2. The ring: _____

_____

_____

3. Sandals: _____

_____

_____

4. The fatted calf: _____

_____

_____

5. The feast and celebration: _____

_____

_____

What was the father's reason for the celebration? (Luke 15:24)

_____

_____

_____

_____

5. **The Elder Brother**

This parable, like the others in Luke 15, was told because the Scribes and Pharisees were complaining that Jesus "welcomes sinners and eats with them." The key to each of the parables is the fact that the shepherd, the woman, and the father rejoiced and celebrated when they found what was lost. Jesus expected the Pharisees and teachers of the law to rejoice also, rather than complain, when "sinners" came to Jesus.

However, since the Pharisees did not seem to get the point in the first two parables, Jesus added a third chapter to this last parable on the prodigal son. He described the attitude of the elder brother, which was the exact attitude of these super-religious people.

What was the elder brother doing when the prodigal returned home? (Luke 15:25)

_____

_____

Since God honors work, the elder brother's activities no doubt pleased his father. The problem, then, is not with what he had been doing, but with his attitude.

What was the attitude of the elder brother? (Luke 15:28)

_____

_____

_____

NOTES

How would you describe this attitude? (Check correct answers.)

_____ Angry

_____ Childish

_____ Selfish

_____ Pouting

_____ Self-righteous

How did the father treat the elder brother? (Luke 15:28)

_____

_____

As we read this parable we discover that both sons were prodigal. One squandered his father's inheritance and was miserable, the other stayed home, kept the rules, and was miserable. The father had to go out to them both. Jesus is pointing out that simply keeping the rules does not make a man happy. He is happy only when he has eyes to see as God sees.

The elder brother was like those Pharisees who were offended because Jesus ate with "sinners." He refused to acknowledge the boy was even his brother.

How did he describe the prodigal son to his father? (Luke 15:30)

_____

In describing his brother's activities in the far country, the elder brother gave a detail the Bible had not mentioned before. Accusing others of things they have not confessed, or of things unproven, is often more of a revelation of the character of the accuser than of the accused.

What did the elder brother accuse the prodigal of having done? (Luke 15:30)

_____

_____

What was the father's reaction to the anger of the elder brother? (Luke 15:31:32)

_____

_____

WRAP UP

All have sinned and come short of God's glory. Keeping the rules does not make us less sinners than squandering all we have in riotous living does. Both the prodigal and the elder brother needed salvation. God does not require anything of us except a broken heart, admission of our sin, and a willingness to come home. He takes care of the rest.

FINAL LESSON

Nothing pleases God, nor should it please us, more than a person who repents and wants to come home.

PERSONAL REVIEW QUESTIONS

Circle T (true) or F (false)

1. T F It's okay to sow my wild oats as a youth because God will always take me in when I get older.

2. T F Sometimes you have to lose everything to find God.

3. T F God does not interfere when we decide to rebel and do things our way.

4. T F God would rather have us back home than have the money we lost in riotious living.

5. T F God is waiting for us to "come to ourselves" and return home.

6. T F God and all the angels rejoice when a lost sinner returns home.

7. T F Religion often keeps us from rejoicing when lost people repent.

8. T F The elder brother was justified in being hurt since he had kept all the rules.

9. T F When we return to God we are totally reinstated as sons.

10. T F God does not put people on probation, but immediately restores them into the family of God.

MEMORY VERSE

I Timothy 1:15 (Memorize, then write it on these lines.)

_____

_____

_____

_____

_____

TRUE OR FALSE ANSWERS:

1-F, 2-T, 3-T, 4-T, 5-T, 6-T, 7-T, 8-F, 9-T, 10-T

NOTES

Information on Ordering

For additional copies of this workbook

or

for the Video Tape Series designed
to be used with the workbook . . .

or

for the other titles in
Jamie Buckingham's Holy Land Series
Ten Miracles of Jesus
Ten Bible People Like Me
Journey to Spiritual Maturity

write or call:
Paraclete Press
P. O. Box 1568
Orleans, MA 02653
Telephone: 1-800-451-5006
or
buy them at your local Christian bookstore.